Better Homes and Gardens®

WOOD™

SMALL FURNITURE

YOU CAN MAKE

=== **WE CARE!** ===

All of us at Meredith® Books are dedicated to giving you the
information and ideas you need to create beautiful and useful
woodworking projects. We guarantee your satisfaction with this
book for as long as you own it. We also welcome your comments
and suggestions. Please write us at Meredith® Books, LS-356SF,
1716 Locust St., Des Moines, IA 50336.

©Copyright 1991 by Meredith Corporation, Des Moines, Iowa. All Rights Reserved. Printed in the United States of America.
First Edition. Printing Number and Year: 5 4   95 94 93 92
Library of Congress Catalog Card Number: 90-64104 ISBN: 0-696-01942-6

A WOOD™ BOOK
Published by Meredith® Books

MEREDITH® BOOKS
Vice President, Editorial Director: Elizabeth P. Rice
Art Director: Ernest Shelton
Managing Editor: David A. Kirchner
Project Editors: James D. Blume, Marsha Jahns
Project Managers: Liz Anderson,
    Jennifer Speer Ramundt, Angela K. Renkoski

Associate Art Directors: Neoma Thomas,
    Linda Ford Vermie, Randall Yontz
Assistant Art Directors: Lynda Haupert, Harijs Priekulis,
    Tom Wegner
Graphic Designers: Mary Schlueter Bendgen,
    Michael Burns, Mick Schnepf
Art Production: Director, John Berg; Associate, Joe Heuer;
    Office Manager, Michaela Lester

President, Book Group: James F. Stack
Vice President, Retail Marketing: Jamie L. Martin
Vice President, Administrative Services: Rick Rundall

WOOD® MAGAZINE
President, Magazine Group: James A. Autry
Editorial Director: Doris Eby
Editor: Larry Clayton

MEREDITH CORPORATION OFFICERS
Chairman of the Executive Committee: E. T. Meredith III
Chairman of the Board: Robert A. Burnett
President and Chief Executive Officer: Jack D. Rehm

SMALL FURNITURE YOU CAN MAKE
Project Editor: James D. Blume
Contributing Project Editor: James A. Hufnagel
Contributing How-To Editor: Marlen Kemmet
Graphic Designers: Mary Schlueter Bendgen, Tom Wegner
Project Manager: Liz Anderson
Contributing Text Editor: Barbara L. Klein
Publishing Systems Text Processor: Paula Forest

Special thanks to Kathy Stevens

On the front cover: Burl-Topped Coffee Table, pages 41–45
On the back cover (clockwise from top left):
    Filigree Plant Stand, pages 8–11; Chippendale Wall
    Mirror, pages 72–75; Walnut Jewelry Case, pages 53–58

Meredith® Books also publishes Better Homes and Gardens® Books,
Country Home™ Books, Meredith® Press Books, and Sedgewood®
Press Books.

SHELVES, STANDS, AND FRAMES

Here we present seven projects that are strictly for show. Display plants, photographs, artwork, and prized collectibles in style with these fun-to-build beauties.

BURL-TOPPED HALLWAY SHELF

Rich-looking walnut, a burl veneer top, and raised-panel craftsmanship make the classic hallway shelf shown *opposite* a real standout.

Build the carcass

1. Referring to the Cutting Diagram, page 7, rip, then crosscut the carcass members (A, B, C, D, E, and F) to the finished sizes indicated in the Bill of Materials, page 7.

2. Using a router and a straight bit, or a tablesaw, cut a ¼" groove ⅜" deep and ¼" from the front edge along the bottom edge of A and B, the top edge of C and D, both edges of E, and both ends of A, B, C, D, and E.

3. Cut the ¼" grooves ⅜" deep along the two adjoining sides of F as shown on the Exploded View Drawing, page 6. Position the grooves ¼" from what will be the two outside faces of F. Using a ¼" cove bit, rout the 4"-long coves on the outside corners of F as dimensioned on the Front View Drawing, *below* . (We clamped stops to our fence and routed the coves in F on the router table.)

4. Rip and crosscut the back carcass member (G) to size, and cut a ⅜" rabbet ⅜" deep along each end.

5. Cut the front and side panels (H and I) to size. (You can buy ½" walnut or resaw ¾" stock to ½" for the panels as we did.) To make the chamfered cuts in H and I, tilt your tablesaw blade 10° from vertical, and raise the blade 1⅜" above the saw-table surface. Set the rip fence ³⁄₁₆" from the blade at table level (see the Panel Section Drawing, *below center*, for reference). Using a pushblock for safety, make the cuts along the edge of each panel. (To avoid costly errors, we test-cut scrap stock first.)

6. Sand all of the cabinet's shell parts, particularly the chamfered borders of the raised panels. Cut the hardboard tenon splines to size as dimensioned on the Exploded View Drawing. Dry-clamp the components together to ensure a precise fit. (To allow for expansion, we planed ¹⁄₁₆" off the top and cut ¹⁄₁₆" off one side edge of each raised panel.) Remove the clamps and make any necessary adjustments.

7. Glue and clamp the cabinet front (A–C–E–F–H). To allow for expansion, H is not glued in the grooves; it floats freely. After drying, glue the end panels to the front assembly and part G between the ends. Clamp and check for square. Remove any excess glue after it develops a tough skin.

8. Cut the trim pieces J and K to size plus 1" in length. Using the top ⅛" of a ³⁄₁₆" round-over bit, rout the front top and bottom edges. Cut J and K to size, mitering both ends of J and the front ends of the Ks. Attach J and K to the bottom of the carcass with glue and brads.

Fashion the shelf top

1. Cut the plywood top (L) to size, and attach the burl veneer (M) with contact cement. Apply contact cement to both the plywood and veneer, then use a veneer roller to flatten out the veneer. Trim veneer flush with the edges of L.

2. Rip the top framing pieces (N, O, and P) and cut them to length, mitering the ends of N and O. Cut a ¼"   *continued*

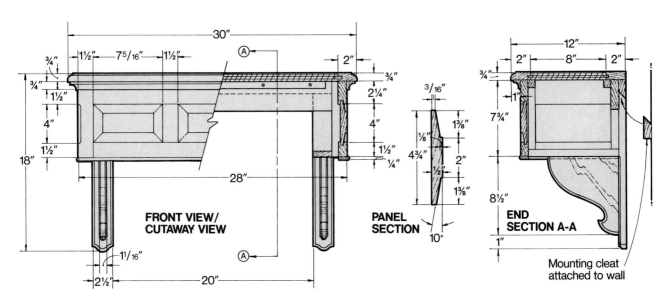

FRONT VIEW/ CUTAWAY VIEW

PANEL SECTION

END SECTION A-A

Mounting cleat attached to wall

BURL-TOPPED HALLWAY SHELF
continued

EXPLODED VIEW

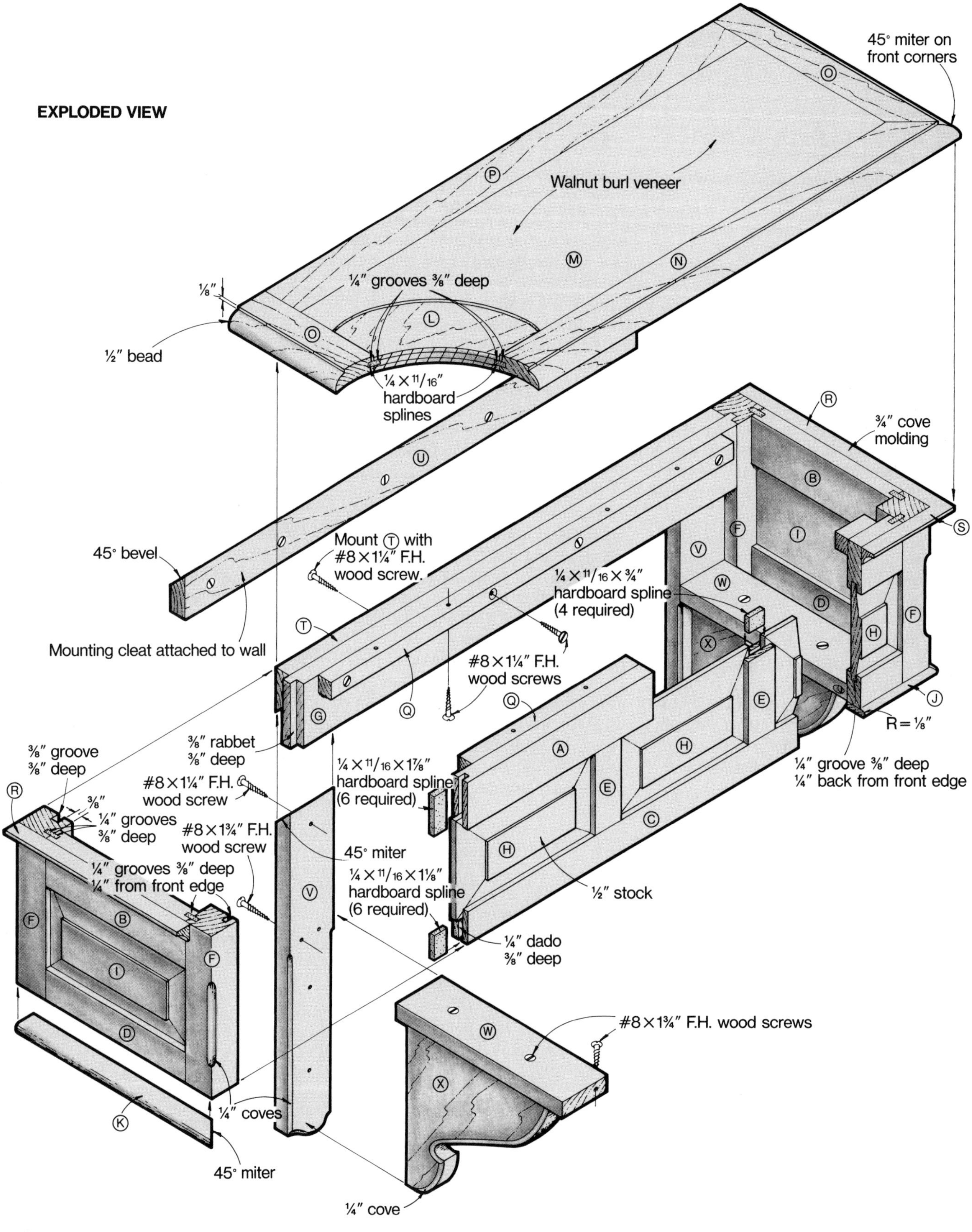
45° miter on front corners
Walnut burl veneer
1/8"
1/4" grooves 3/8" deep
1/2" bead
1/4 × 11/16" hardboard splines
3/4" cove molding
45° bevel
Mount T with #8 × 1 1/4" F.H. wood screw.
1/4 × 11/16 × 3/4" hardboard spline (4 required)
Mounting cleat attached to wall
#8 × 1 1/4" F.H. wood screws
R = 1/8"
1/4" groove 3/8" deep 1/4" back from front edge
3/8" groove 3/8" deep
3/8" rabbet 3/8" deep
#8 × 1 1/4" F.H. wood screw
1/4 × 11/16 × 1 7/8" hardboard spline (6 required)
3/8"
1/4" grooves 3/8" deep
#8 × 1 3/4" F.H. wood screw
45° miter
1/4" grooves 3/8" deep 1/4" from front edge
1/4 × 11/16 × 1 1/8" hardboard spline (6 required)
1/2" stock
1/4" dado 3/8" deep
#8 × 1 3/4" F.H. wood screws
1/4" coves
45° miter
1/4" cove

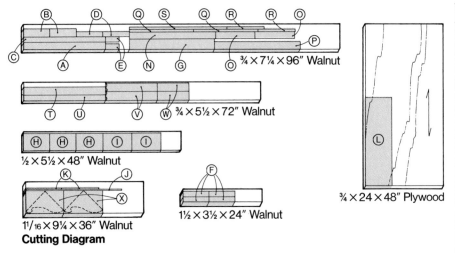

¾ × 7¼ × 96" Walnut

¾ × 5½ × 72" Walnut

½ × 5½ × 48" Walnut

1¹/₁₆ × 9¼ × 36" Walnut

1½ × 3½ × 24" Walnut

¾ × 24 × 48" Plywood

Cutting Diagram

Bill of Materials

Part	T	W	L	Mat.	Qty.
	Finished Size*				
A carcass member	¾"	2¼"	25"	W	1
B carcass member	¾"	2¼"	8"	W	2
C carcass member	¾"	1½"	25"	W	1
D carcass member	¾"	1½"	8"	W	2
E carcass member	¾"	1½"	4"	W	2
F carcass member	1½"	1½"	7¾"	W	4
G back carcass	¾"	3"	25¾"	W	1
H front panel	½"	4¾"	8¹/₁₆"	W	3
I side panel	½"	4¾"	8¾"	W	2
J* trim	¼"	1"	28½"	W	1
K* trim	¼"	1"	11¼"	W	2
L top	¾"	8"	26"	PLY	1
M* veneer	¹/₂₈"	8"	26"	WBV	1
N top frame	¾"	2"	30"	W	1
O top frame	¾"	2"	12"	W	2
P top frame	¾"	2"	26"	W	1
Q top cleat	¾"	¾"	23½"	P	2
R cove molding	¾"	¾"	11¾"	W	2
S cove molding	¾"	¾"	29½"	W	1
T mounting cleat	¾"	2"	25"	W	1
U mounting cleat	¾"	2"	19½"	W	1
V bracket member	¾"	2½"	15⅝"	W	2
W bracket member	¾"	2½"	9½"	W	2
X bracket member	1¹/₁₆"	8"	8½"	W	2

*Parts marked with an * are cut larger initially, then trimmed to finished size. Please read the instructions before cutting.

Material Key: W—walnut, PLY—plywood, WBV—walnut burl veneer, P—pine.

Supplies: contact cement, #8 × 1¼" flathead wood screws, #8 × 1½" flathead wood screws, #8 × 1¾" flathead wood screws, ¼" hardboard for splines, ½" brads, finish.

groove ⅜" deep along the center of the inside edge of N, O, and P and the ends of P. To ensure a flat top, machine all pieces with the top side against the fence. Using the same setting, cut the ¼" groove ⅜" in the L-M panel. Cut ¼" hardboard splines to size.

3. Glue and clamp the top assembly together. When dry, use a ½" round-over bit to rout a bead along the front and side edges of the top as indicated on the Exploded View Drawing.

4. Rip, then crosscut the top cleats (Q) to size. Place the assembled top upside down on a work surface and position the carcass on the top as dimensioned. Hold the back cleat against G, then drill and countersink pilot holes where indicated and install the screws. Repeat this process to attach the front cleat to A.

5. Drill pilot holes through Q into the top (L), and attach the top to the carcass with #8 × 1¼" screws. Cut the cove molding pieces (R and S) to size, mitering both ends of S and the front end of R. Attach to the underside of the top lip with glue and brads.

6. Rip a piece of ¾" walnut to 4" and crosscut it to 25", then bevel-rip it in half at 45° to form parts T and U. Attach T to the back of the cabinet assembly as shown on the End Section A–A Drawing, page 5. Cut U to 19½". You will later screw part U to the

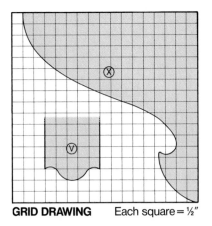

GRID DRAWING   Each square = ½"

wall to interlock with T, thus mounting the shelf to the wall.

Make the shelf brackets

1. Cut the bracket members (V, W, X) to size and shape as indicated on the Grid Pattern Drawing, *above,* and the End Section A–A Drawing. Use a ¼" cove bit to rout the decorative edges on V and X. Assemble the brackets as shown on the Exploded View Drawing.

2. Attach the bracket member assembly to the shelf, toe-screwing W to A and screwing V to the back of G. Finish-sand the shelf, being careful not to sand through the veneer, then apply the finish of your choice. (We applied polyurethane, using steel wool between coats.) Attach part U to the wall and mount the shelf, interlocking T and U as described in step 6 of the section "Fashion the shelf top."

FILIGREE PLANT STAND

J im Boelling, our project
builder, started experi-
menting with laser-cut filigree
and came up with this classic-
looking stand. (For our source
of filigree, check out the
Buying Guide, page 11.)

Shape up the legs

1. Cut the legs (A) to the size
listed in the Bill of Materials. We
used 1 1/16"-thick birch (commonly called 5/4 stock) for the legs. If
you have trouble locating stock
this size, you can laminate 3/4"
stock face-to-face, and then resaw
or plane the laminations to the
correct thickness. Be sure to
plane or resaw an equal amount
off each face so the glue line
remains exactly centered.

2. Rout a 3/16" round-over along
all four edges of each leg. (We
did this on a table-mounted
router fitted with a fence to avoid
routing the top and bottom ends
of the legs—the ends need to
remain flat.)

3. Sand a slight round-over on
the bottom of each leg to prevent
the leg from later snagging the
carpet. Sand each leg.

Construct the apron frames

1. Crosscut a 3/4"-thick piece of
birch to 24" in length. Now rip
four 1/2"-wide strips from the 24"-
long piece. Each strip should
measure 1/2 × 3/4 × 24" for the
apron-frame members (B, C).

2. To form the 1/2" bullnose,
rout 1/4" round-overs on the top
and bottom corners of one edge
of each 24" strip. See the Rail
Detail, *opposite, bottom.*

3. Cut a 1/8" groove 1/8" deep
along each 24"-long strip where
shown on the Rail Detail to house

the laser-cut filigree. Sand the
four strips.

4. Set a stop for consistent
lengths, and miter-cut eight rails
(B) to length from the 24"-long
strips. Reposition the stop and cut
eight stiles (C) to length. (For
minimum waste, we cut two rails
and two stiles from each strip.)

5. Cut the filigree to length,
being sure to center the laser-cut
pattern in each apron frame. To
do this, start by marking a
centerline across one frame rail
(B). Insert the filigree into the 1/8"
groove in the rail, and center one
of the filigree circles directly over

the marked line as shown in
photo A, *opposite, top left.* Mark
the ends of the filigree where
shown on the photo, and crosscut
the four filigree strips to length.
(Our strips measured 7 3/8" long.)

6. Tape together (no glue just
yet) each apron frame (with the
filigree in place in the grooved
opening) to check the fit of all
the pieces. (When checking the
fit of small parts such as these, we
found that masking tape works
better than clamps.) Remove the
tape, and trim parts if necessary.
Glue and tape each frame,
checking for square and tight

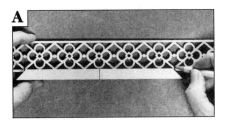

A

Center the filigree over the marked centerline, and mark cutlines for matching patterns at each end.

joints. Wipe off excess glue with a damp cloth.

7. Snip the head end off a #17×¾" brad, and chuck it into a portable drill. Use the brad bit to drill pilot holes where shown on the Rail Detail, *below.* Drive #17×¾" brads into the pilot holes to strengthen the joints.

Attach the legs

1. Cut two pieces of scrap stock to the same length as the apron rails. *continued*

Cutting Diagram

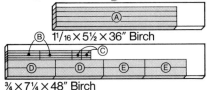

Ⓐ
1¹/₁₆ × 5½ × 36" Birch

Ⓑ Ⓒ
Ⓓ Ⓓ Ⓔ Ⓔ
¾ × 7¼ × 48" Birch
Note: Ⓕ is cut from ¼" birch plywood.

EXPLODED VIEW

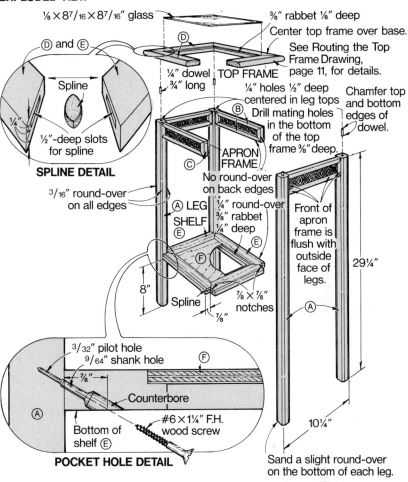

⅛ × 8⁷/₁₆ × 8⁷/₁₆" glass

⅜" rabbet ⅛" deep
Center top frame over base.
See Routing the Top Frame Drawing, page 11, for details.

Ⓓ and Ⓔ

Spline

¼"

½"-deep slots for spline

SPLINE DETAIL

³/₁₆" round-over on all edges

Ⓓ TOP FRAME

¼" dowel ¾" long

¼" holes ½" deep centered in leg tops
Ⓑ Drill mating holes in the bottom of the top frame ⅜" deep.

Chamfer top and bottom edges of dowel.

Ⓒ APRON FRAME

No round-over on back edges

Ⓐ LEG

¼" round-over
⅜" rabbet ¼" deep

SHELF
Ⓔ

Ⓕ

Front of apron frame is flush with outside face of legs.

8"

Spline

⅞ × ⅞" notches

⅞"

29¼"

Ⓐ

10¼"

Sand a slight round-over on the bottom of each leg.

POCKET HOLE DETAIL

³/₃₂" pilot hole
⁹/₆₄" shank hole
⅞"
Ⓕ
Counterbore
Ⓐ
Bottom of shelf Ⓔ
#6×1¼" F.H. wood screw

RAIL DETAIL

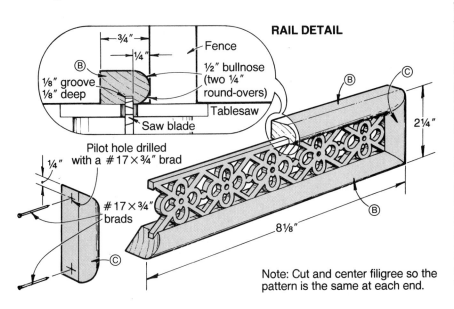

¾"
¼"
Fence
Ⓑ
⅛" groove
⅛" deep
½" bullnose (two ¼" round-overs)
Tablesaw
Saw blade

Pilot hole drilled with a #17×¾" brad

¼"

#17×¾" brads

Ⓒ

Ⓑ Ⓒ

2¼"

Ⓑ

8⅛"

Note: Cut and center filigree so the pattern is the same at each end.

Bill of Materials

Part	Finished Size*			Mat.	Qty.
	T	W	L		
A leg	1¹/₁₆"	1¹/₁₆"	29¼"	B	4
B* rail	½"	¾"	8⅛"	B	8
C* stile	½"	¾"	2¼"	B	8
D* top member	¾"	2"	11¾"	B	4
E* shelf member	¾"	2"	9⅞"	B	4
F shelf panel	¼"	6⅝"	6⅝"	BP	1

*Parts marked with an * are cut larger initially, then trimmed to finished size. Please read the instructions before cutting.

Material Key: B—birch, BP—birch plywood.
Supplies: #6×1¼" flathead wood screws, ¼" dowel, #17×¾" brads, ⅛ × 8⁷/₁₆ × 8⁷/₁₆" double-strength glass, stain, finish.

9

FILIGREE PLANT STAND
continued

2. As shown in photo B, *opposite,* lay the legs and apron frame facedown. Glue and clamp the pieces, using the scrap piece at the opposite end of the legs as a spacer. Check that the top of the apron frame is flush with the top ends of the legs and that the front of the apron frame is flush with the front of the legs. (We found that laying the pieces facedown helped keep the front edges flush.) Repeat the process with the two remaining legs and one of the apron frames.

3. Glue and clamp the remaining two apron frames between the two leg-frame assemblies. Check that the tops and fronts are flush, and that the assembly is square. Immediately wipe off any excess glue with a damp cloth.

Build the top and shelf

1. From ¾"-thick birch stock, rip and crosscut two strips 2" wide by 48" long.

2. Miter-cut the four top members (D) and the four shelf members (E) to length, setting stops for consistent lengths. (Cut two Ds and two Es from each 48" strip.)

3. To form the guide block shown on Step 1 of the Routing the Slots Drawing, *above right,* cut an 8"-square piece of ¾"-thick scrap stock. Draw a diagonal line (corner to corner), and cut the square in half.

4. To make the stopblock shown on Step 2 of the Routing the Slots Drawing, cut a piece of ¾" stock to 2" wide by 11" long. Miter-cut one end at 45°.

5. Mount a ¼" slot cutter and fence to your table-mounted router. Raise the slot cutter to cut a slot centered on the edge of the ¾" stock. Position the router-table fence so the slot cutter bearing is flush with the front face of the fence where shown on Step 1. Finally, mark the three reference

lines on the fence where dimensioned on Step 1.

6. Clamp the guide block and stopblock to the router table, aligning the pieces with the marked reference lines where shown on Step 2. Cut a test strip of ¾"-thick stock to 2" wide, and miter-cut one end at 45°. Cut a ¼" slot ½" deep in the mitered end of the test strip. Check that the slot is centered from left to right and top to bottom as shown on the Spline Detail accompanying the Exploded View Drawing on page 9. Make adjustments as necessary. Cut a slot on one end of each birch frame member (D, E) where shown on Step 2. For flush-fitting joints, keep the same face down and rout the opposite end of each frame member where shown on Step 3.

7. Using the Full-Sized Spline Pattern, *below,* as a guide, mark and cut one spline to shape from

FULL-SIZED SPLINE PATTERN

¼" hardboard. Test-fit (no glue) the spline between two frame members. Adjust the spline if necessary. Using this first spline as a template, mark and cut 7 more splines to shape. Sand a slight chamfer along the top and bottom edges of each spline.

8. Dry-clamp the top frame together to check for square and tight-fitting joints. Trim if necessary. Then glue and clamp the top-frame pieces together, checking for square. Remove the clamps, and sand the frame smooth. Repeat the process to form the shelf.

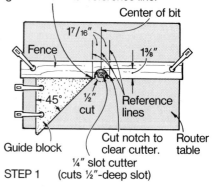

ROUTING THE SLOTS
Position and clamp corner of guide block with reference line.

Center of bit

1⁷⁄₁₆"

Fence

1⅜"

45°
½"
cut

Reference lines

Cut notch to clear cutter.

Guide block

Router table

¼" slot cutter (cuts ½"-deep slot)

STEP 1

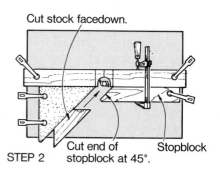

Cut stock facedown.

Cut end of stopblock at 45°.

Stopblock

STEP 2

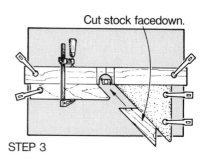

Cut stock facedown.

STEP 3

9. Following the Routing the Top Frame Drawing, *opposite, top left,* rout the top and bottom edges of the top frame.

10. Rout a ¼" round-over along the top edges of the shelf. Switch to a rabbeting bit, and rout a ⅜" rabbet ¼" deep along the top inside edges of the shelf frame. Reset the depth of the cut, and rout a ⅜" rabbet ⅛" deep into the top inside edge of the top frame.

ROUTING THE TOP FRAME

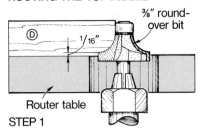

⅜" round-over bit

D

1/16"

Router table

STEP 1

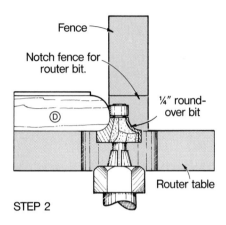

Fence

Notch fence for router bit.

D

¼" round-over bit

Router table

STEP 2

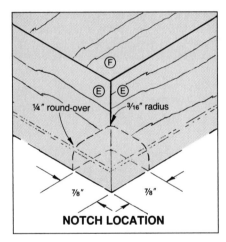

F

E E

¼" round-over

³⁄₁₆" radius

⅞" ⅞"

NOTCH LOCATION

11. Square the inside corners of the shelf frame and top frame with a chisel. Cut a piece of ¼" birch plywood (F) to fit the rabbeted recess in the shelf. Glue and clamp the plywood panel in the shelf. Later, carefully sand smooth.

12. Using a square, mark a ⅞ × ⅞" notch on each corner of the bottom side of the shelf. Then mark a ³⁄₁₆" radius on the inside corner of each notch where shown on the Notch Location

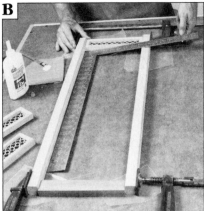

B

Glue and clamp an apron frame between two legs, using a spacer to keep the legs parallel. Check the assembly for square.

C

Mark a centerpoint ⅞" from the notch on the miter-joint line, and drill ⅛" deep.

D

Angle the drill and drill a counter-bored hole through the shelf and into the plant stand leg.

Drawing, *center far left.* Cut the notches to shape.

Attach the shelf and top

1. Turn the plant stand upside down. Make a mark on each leg 8" from the bottom end of each leg. Position the shelf so that the bottom face of the shelf aligns with the marked lines. Clamp the shelf (also upside down) in position as shown in photo C, *middle left.* Check that the shelf is flush with the marked lines.

2. Using the Pocket Hole Detail accompanying the Exploded View Drawing as a guide, mark an X on the miter joint ⅞" from the inside corner of each notch. To start the pocket hole, drill straight down ⅛" as shown in photo B. (We used a Stanley 1" × #6 Screw Sink.)

3. Tilt the drill, and drill into the leg (A) as shown in photo D, *bottom left.* Install the screw. Repeat the drilling and screwing operation at each corner. Remove the clamps.

4. Mark diagonals and drill ¼" holes ½" deep into the top end of each leg. Place a ¼" dowel center in each hole. Center the top frame on the legs, and press down to transfer the dowel-hole centers to the bottom side of the top frame. Drill ¼" holes ⅜" deep into the bottom face of the top frame where marked.

5. Cut four ¼" dowels to ¾" in length. Sand a chamfer on each end of each dowel. Glue and dowel the top frame to the leg assembly. Remove excess glue.

Sand and finish

1. Finish-sand the entire stand and apply the stain. Brush on two coats of clear finish.

2. Take the stand to a glass dealer, and order the glass top.

Buying Guide

• **Laser-cut filigree.** ⅛"-thick, white maple ply with a poplar core, 36" long. Catalog no. FIL8-WD. For current price, contact Constantine's, 2050 Eastchester Rd., Bronx, NY 10461. Or call 800-223-8087.

COLLECTOR'S SHOWCASE

It doesn't take a Philadelphia lawyer to make a case for this project. For opening arguments, we offer simple dowel joints to form the sturdy case as well as spline-mitered doors. Here are the facts: From first cut to the first coat of finish, it took us less than eight hours to build with only a modest investment in materials. What's the verdict? The jury declares this another prizewinning project.

Construct the case

1. Rip and crosscut the case sides (A) and top and bottom (B) to the sizes listed in the Bill of Materials.

2. Follow the Routing the Edges Drawing, *below right*, to rout the front edges and ends of the top and bottom pieces (B).

3. Mark the dowel-hole centerpoints on the ends of each case side where shown on the Hole Detail accompanying the Exploded View Drawing, *opposite.* Using a doweling jig, drill ⅜″ holes ⁹⁄₁₆″ deep.

4. Place dowel centers in the holes just drilled. Center the sides (A) between the top and bottom (B) where shown on the Exploded View Drawing. Clamp together the pieces to transfer the hole locations to the top and bottom pieces. (Depending on how many dowel centers you have, you might have to do one joint at a time.) Transfer the ⅜″ bit to your drill press, and drill ⅜″ holes ⁹⁄₁₆″ deep where marked.

5. Sand the four pieces. Using ⅜″ dowel pins 1″ long, glue, dowel, and clamp the sides between the top and bottom pieces, checking for square. Immediately remove excess glue.

6. To house the back (C), rout a ⅜″ rabbet ¼″ deep along the back inside edge *continued*

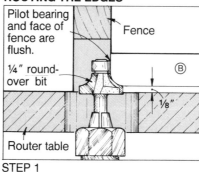

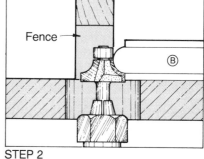

Display thimbles, spoons, or other small collectibles in this classy cabinet.

Cutting Diagram

*Note: Plane or resaw splines to ⅛″ thick and shelves Ⓓ to ½″ thick.

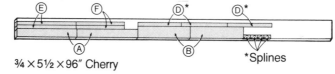

¾ × 5½ × 96″ Cherry

*Splines

¼ × 24 × 24″
Cherry Plywood

ROUTING THE EDGES

Pilot bearing and face of fence are flush.

¼″ round-over bit

Fence

Ⓑ

⅛″

Router table

STEP 1

Fence

Ⓑ

STEP 2

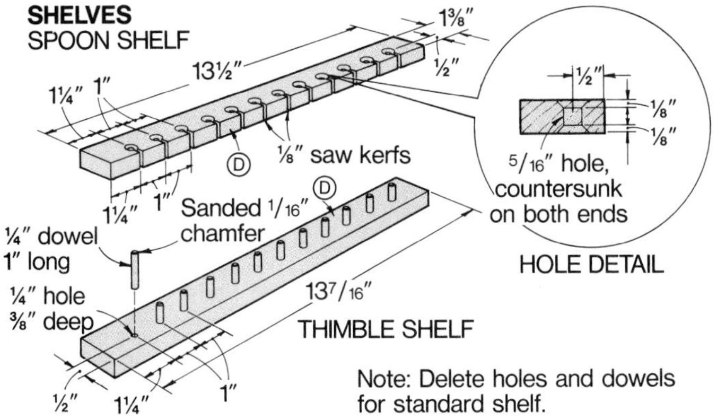

SHELVES
SPOON SHELF
1⅜″
13½″
½″
1¼″ 1″
⅛″ saw kerfs
Ⓓ
1¼″ 1″
Sanded 1/16″ chamfer
¼″ dowel 1″ long
¼″ hole ⅜″ deep
13 7/16″
THIMBLE SHELF
½″ 1¼″ 1″
½″
⅛″
⅛″
5/16″ hole, countersunk on both ends
HOLE DETAIL
Note: Delete holes and dowels for standard shelf.

Bill of Materials					
Part	Finished Size*			Mat.	Qty.
	T	W	L		
Case					
A side	¾″	2¾″	18½″	C	2
B top/ bottom	¾″	3⅞″	16″	C	2
C back	¼″	14¼″	19¼″	CP	1
D shelf	½″	1⅜″	13 7/16″	C	3/5
Door					
E* stile	¾″	1″	18⅜″	C	2
F* rail	¾″	1″	15″	C	2

*Parts marked with an * are cut larger initially, then trimmed to finished size. Please read the instructions before cutting.

Material Key: C—cherry, CP—cherry plywood.

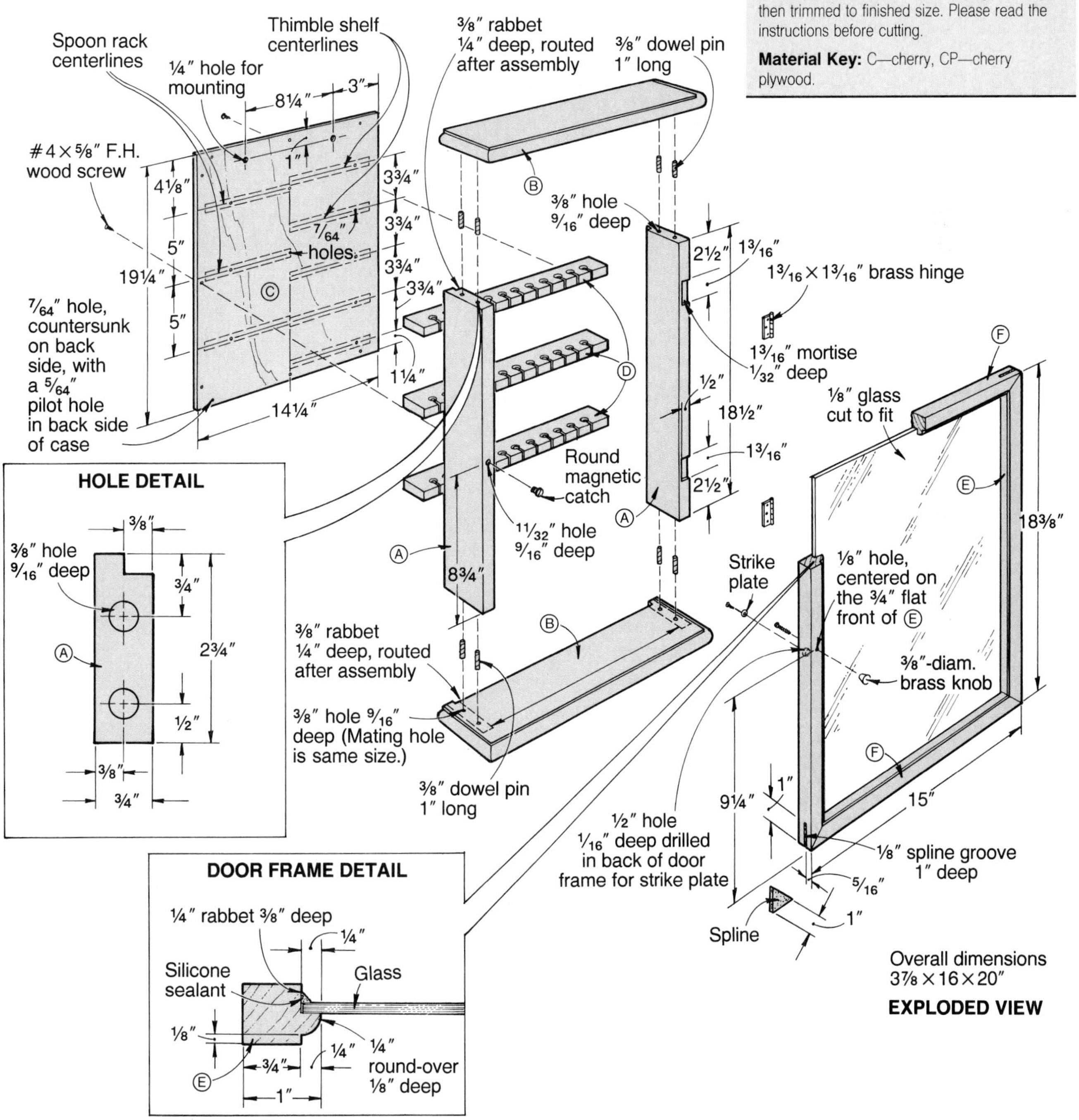

Spoon rack centerlines
Thimble shelf centerlines
¼″ hole for mounting
8¼″
3″
1″
⅜″ rabbet ¼″ deep, routed after assembly
⅜″ dowel pin 1″ long
#4×⅝″ F.H. wood screw
4⅛″
3¾″
3¾″
3¾″
3¾″
7/64″ holes
5″
5″
19¼″
Ⓒ
14¼″
1¼″
7/64″ hole, countersunk on back side, with a 5/64″ pilot hole in back side of case
Ⓑ
⅜″ hole 9/16″ deep
2½″
13/16″
13/16×13/16″ brass hinge
13/16″ mortise 1/32″ deep
Ⓓ
½″
18½″
13/16″
2½″
Ⓐ
Round magnetic catch
11/32″ hole 9/16″ deep
8¾″
Ⓐ
Ⓕ
⅛″ glass cut to fit
Ⓔ
18⅜″
Strike plate
⅛″ hole, centered on the ¾″ flat front of Ⓔ
⅜″-diam. brass knob
Ⓑ
⅜″ rabbet ¼″ deep, routed after assembly
⅜″ hole 9/16″ deep (Mating hole is same size.)
⅜″ dowel pin 1″ long
Ⓕ
15″
9¼″
1″
½″ hole 1/16″ deep drilled in back of door frame for strike plate
⅛″ spline groove 1″ deep
5/16″
1″
Spline
HOLE DETAIL
⅜″
⅜″ hole 9/16″ deep
¾″
2¾″
Ⓐ
½″
⅜″
¾″
DOOR FRAME DETAIL
¼″ rabbet ⅜″ deep
¼″
Silicone sealant
Glass
⅛″
¾″
¼″
¼″ round-over ⅛″ deep
1″
Ⓔ
Overall dimensions 3⅞×16×20″
EXPLODED VIEW

COLLECTOR'S SHOWCASE
continued

of the case frame (A, B). Square the corners with a chisel.

7. Cut the back (C) to size. Drill the mounting holes in the back and case, and screw the back in place.

Make the shelves of your choice

1. Cut the shelves (D) to size from ½" stock (we resawed ¾" stock to size). You'll need three shelves for spoons or five shelves for thimbles.

2. For the spoon shelves, mark the hole centerpoints where dimensioned on the Shelves Drawing, page 13. Drill and countersink a 5⁄16" hole at each centerpoint (refer to the Hole Detail accompanying the Shelves Drawing). Flip over the piece and countersink the holes on the opposite surface.

3. With a combination square, mark the kerf locations centered on the holes just drilled. Attach an auxiliary fence to your miter gauge. Raise your blade ½" above the saw table, and cut the kerfs where marked as shown in photo A, *upper right.*

4. To build the thimble shelves, mark the dowel-hole centerpoints on five shelves where shown on the Shelves Drawing. Using a brad-point or Forstner bit, drill twelve ¼" holes ⅜" deep where marked in each shelf. (To ensure consistent hole depths, we set the depth stop on our drill press. And, to keep the holes in a straight line, we clamped a fence to our drill-press table.)

5. Cut sixty ¼" dowels 1" long for the thimble posts. Finish-sand each shelf smooth, then sand a slight chamfer on both ends of each dowel. Place a drop of glue in each hole, and tap the dowels into place. Immediately wipe off excess glue with a damp cloth.

Mount an auxiliary fence to your miter gauge, and cut the kerfs.

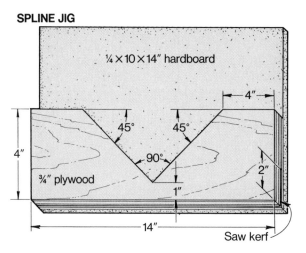

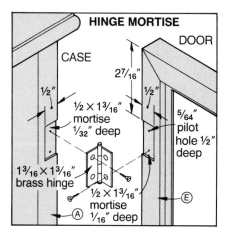

6. Using double-faced tape, adhere the shelves in position in the case. Drill the 7⁄64" shank holes through the back (C) and 5⁄64" pilot holes ½" deep into the shelves where shown on the Exploded View Drawing, page 13. Remove the shelves and double-faced tape. (We attached the shelves to the back after staining.) Now drill a pair of ¼" holes through the case back, where shown on the Exploded View Drawing, for later mounting of the completed case to a wall.

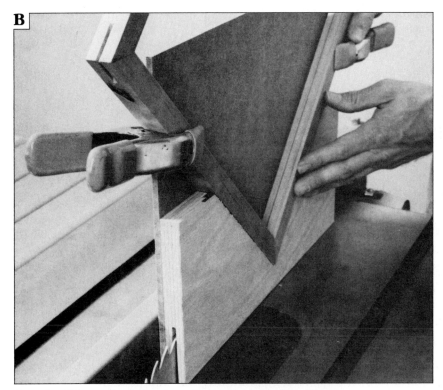

B

Cut a kerf through each mitered corner of the door frame.

Build the door

1. Cut two pieces of ¾"-thick cherry to 1" wide by 20" long for the door stiles (E) and two more pieces 1" wide by 16" long for the rails (F).

2. Referring to the Door Frame Detail accompanying the Exploded View Drawing, rout a ¼" round-over along the front inside edge of each door piece. Cut or rout a ¼" rabbet ⅜" deep along the back inside edge to house the glass.

3. Miter-cut the stiles (E) and rails (F) to the lengths listed in the Bill of Materials, page 13. (For extra support, we attached an auxiliary fence to our miter gauge and mitered the pieces to length on the tablesaw.)

4. With the surfaces flush, glue and clamp together the door frame, checking for square.

5. Build a spline jig to the dimensions shown on the Spline Jig Drawing, *opposite, middle.* Raise the blade 2" above the tablesaw surface. Now, as shown in photo B, *above,* cut a ⅛" kerf 1" deep in each corner of the door frame.

6. Cut a piece of ⅛" cherry (we resawed a thicker piece) to 1¼" wide by 12" long. Next, cut four slip-feather splines to 2⅛" long (see the Full-Sized Spline Drawing, *opposite*). Glue a spline in each kerfed corner of the frame. When dry, trim or sand off the protruding spline, being careful not to cut or sand the door frame.

Attach the hardware

1. Mark the hinge locations on the right side piece (A) where shown on the Hinge Mortise Drawing, *opposite, bottom.* Using double-faced tape, adhere the hinges to the side piece. With an awl, poke through the tape and screw holes in the hinge and into the side piece. Next, drill the hinge mounting holes.

2. With a hobby knife, score the outline of the hinges. Remove the hinges and tape. Using a sharp chisel, form a pair of ¹⁄₃₂"-deep mortises in the side piece (A), cutting to the scored outlines. Screw the hinges to the side piece.

3. Repeat the process in steps 1 and 2 to form a pair of ¹⁄₁₆"-deep mortises in the door.

4. Drill the mounting hole for the magnetic catch where shown on the Exploded View Drawing. To fasten the strike plate to the mating location on the back side of the door, drill a ½" hole ¹⁄₁₆" deep with a ⁵⁄₆₄" pilot hole centered inside.

5. Drill the ⅛" mounting hole, and attach the knob where shown on the Exploded View Drawing.

Remove the hardware and apply the finish

1. Remove the hinges, magnetic catch, strike plate, and knob. Finish-sand all the parts.

2. Wipe on the stain. Using ¾" wood screws, fasten the shelves to the plywood back. Apply the finish of your choice.

3. Have a piece of ⅛" glass cut to fit the door frame. (We secured the glass in the door frame with a fine bead of clear silicone sealant.)

4. Attach the hardware and door. Place the back into the rabbeted opening, drill the holes, and then screw the back in place. Level the case and then fasten it to the wall.

Buying Guide
• **Hardware kit.** 1³⁄₁₆ × 1³⁄₁₆" solid-brass butt hinges, ⅜"-diameter polished knob, magnetic catch. Kit no. 71042. For current price, contact Klockit, P.O. Box 636, Lake Geneva, WI 53147. Or call 800-556-2548.

PEDESTAL DISPLAY STAND

E ven a lush fern takes a
backseat to this graceful
pedestal table. The black walnut
brings a richness that
complements the decor of any
room. But the real joy comes
from developing your turning
skills on a project that yields
impressive results. Be careful,
though—lathe work can
become very addictive!

Build the top
1. Rip, then crosscut enough
¾″ walnut boards to make a 15″
square for the top (A). Glue and
clamp the boards, checking that
the top surface of the boards is
absolutely flush.

2. After the glue dries, remove
the clamps, scrape off any excess
glue, and sand smooth. On the
bottom, draw diagonal lines from
corner to corner to find the
center of the square, and use a
compass to mark a 7″ radius. (If
you don't have a compass large
enough to mark a 7″ radius, cut a
piece of scrap and drive a nail
through one end. Seven inches
from the nail, drill a hole large
enough for the lead of your
pencil. Center the nail on the
bottom of the tabletop and mark
the circle.) Now mark a 2½″
radius for the mounting ring on
the bottom of the tabletop.

3. Cut the top to shape, then
sand the edge smooth. (We cut
slightly outside the cutoff line
with a bandsaw, then used a disc
sander to finish shaping.)

4. Glue up a 6″ walnut square
for the mounting ring (B), then
mark its center and scribe a 2½″
radius. Cut and sand it to shape
as you did the tabletop. Bore a 1″
hole through the centerpoint of
the mounting ring. Now drill four
pilot holes through the mounting
ring for the screws that will
fasten it to the top.

5. Rout the bead along the top
edge of the tabletop with a ½″
round-over bit. Switch to a ⅜″
round-over bit and rout the
bottom of the mounting ring.

Turn the pedestal
1. Square up a 3″ turning
square, then trim it to a finished
length of 15¼″ for the pedestal
(C). If you don't have 3″-square
stock, laminate thinner stock to
that size.

2. Mark diagonal lines to find
the center of each end, then
center-punch each end and

mount the square onto the lathe.

3. Scribe a pencil mark 3″ from
the end of the square nearest the
headstock. Starting at the 3″ mark,
turn the pedestal to its finished
shape, referring to the Turning
Profile Drawing, *opposite, center,*
as a guide.

Build the legs
1. Enlarge the Leg Grid Pattern,
opposite, right, and lay out the
shape of one leg (D) on a piece
of walnut as shown. Now cut one
leg to shape, sand out the saw
marks, and use it as a template to

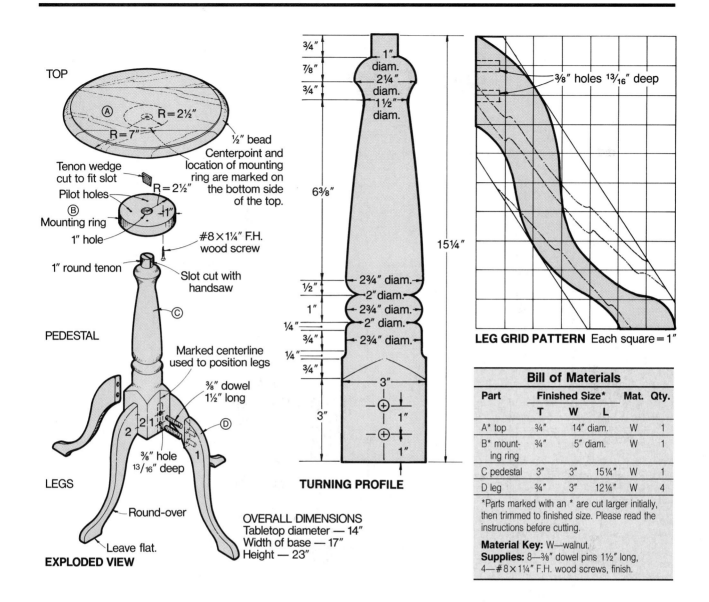

TOP

R = 2½"
R = 7"
Ⓐ

Tenon wedge cut to fit slot
Pilot holes
Ⓑ
Mounting ring
1" hole
R = 2½"
1"

½" bead
Centerpoint and location of mounting ring are marked on the bottom side of the top.

#8 × 1¼" F.H. wood screw

1" round tenon
Slot cut with handsaw

Ⓒ

PEDESTAL

Marked centerline used to position legs

⅜" dowel 1½" long

Ⓓ

2 1
2   1
1

⅜" hole 13/16" deep

LEGS

Round-over

Leave flat.

EXPLODED VIEW

TURNING PROFILE

¾"
1" diam.
⅞"
2¼" diam.
¾"
1½" diam.
6⅜"
15¼"
½"
2¾" diam.
2" diam.
1"
2¾" diam.
¼"
2" diam.
¾"
2¾" diam.
¼"
¾"
3"
1"
3"
1"

OVERALL DIMENSIONS
Tabletop diameter — 14"
Width of base — 17"
Height — 23"

⅜" holes 13/16" deep

LEG GRID PATTERN Each square = 1"

Bill of Materials				
Part	**Finished Size***		**Mat.**	**Qty.**
	T	**W** **L**		
A* top	¾"	14" diam.	W	1
B* mounting ring	¾"	5" diam.	W	1
C pedestal	3"	3" 15¼"	W	1
D leg	¾"	3" 12¼"	W	4

*Parts marked with an * are cut larger initially, then trimmed to finished size. Please read the instructions before cutting.

Material Key: W—walnut.
Supplies: 8—⅜" dowel pins 1½" long, 4—#8 × 1¼" F.H. wood screws, finish.

Cutting Diagram

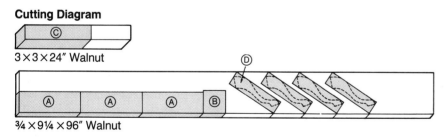

Ⓒ
3 × 3 × 24" Walnut

Ⓓ
Ⓐ   Ⓐ   Ⓐ   Ⓑ
¾ × 9¼ × 96" Walnut

mark the remaining legs. Cut the legs to shape.

2. Using double-faced tape, tape all four legs together, edges flush. Clamp the legs together to ensure that all the pieces are firmly secured to one another.

3. Contour-sand the edges of the legs until all four legs are a uniform shape. Remove the clamps and tape from the legs.

4. Reference-mark each leg with a numeral (1, 2, 3, or 4), then place corresponding marks on the pedestal. This will enable you to later match each leg to its corresponding side of the pedestal.   *continued*

PEDESTAL DISPLAY STAND
continued

Scribe the vertical center of each face of the squared portion of the pedestal as shown on the Exploded View Drawing, page 17. Now mark the center of the mating surface of each leg.

5. Drill two ⅜" dowel holes 1³⁄₁₆" deep into each leg and insert a ⅜" dowel center in each hole. Align each leg with its corresponding side on the pedestal and squeeze together to mark the location of the dowel holes on the pedestal. Drill ⅜" holes ⅞" deep in the pedestal, then sand the legs smooth.

6. Using a ⅜" round-over bit, rout all edges of the legs except the bottom edge where the leg meets the floor and the top edge where the leg connects to the pedestal.

7. Trial-fit the legs into their respective holes and set the table base on a perfectly flat surface. If it tilts, see the tip at *right* to learn how to level the legs. Once the table sits level, glue, dowel, and clamp the legs to the pedestal as shown in the photo *below*.

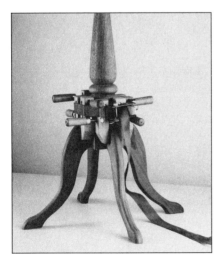

Complete the assembly
1. Using a handsaw, cut a slot in the center of the tenon end of the pedestal and a wedge to fit the slot. The wedge should just

slightly expand the tenon, yet firmly hold the ring (B) in position. Carefully sand the wedge to shape.

2. Fit the ring onto the tenon, then glue and drive the wedge into position.

3. Finish-sand all the parts and screw the pedestal to the top. Finish as desired.

How to Level a Wobbly Project

Use our technique to level a piece with four or more legs. In a three-legged piece, the single offending leg obviously is easier to identify and remedy.

First, remove any glides or cushions from the bottoms of the legs. Then place the piece on a level work surface and set your level on the tabletop or chair seat so that the level points toward two directly opposite legs.

Shim beneath the legs as necessary until the top surface reads level, then rotate your level 90°. Check for level again and shim as needed. Now shift your level back to the original position to make sure it's still true there.

Next measure the gap between the work surface and the bottom of the leg that's the farthest above that surface. Make a shim about ¹⁄₁₆" thicker than the gap is wide and place a pencil on its side atop the shim. Mark a line along the bottom of each leg (see photo A, *top right*) to determine where you need to cut in order to level the project.

Lay the entire project on its side and cut the bottom of each offending leg with a jigsaw or handsaw (we use a clamped-on piece of scrapwood as a guide—see photo B, *bottom right*).

When your level indicates satisfactory results, touch up the

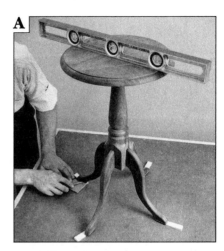

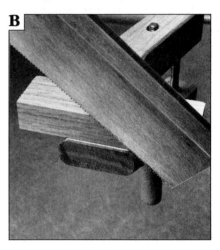

project by smooth-sanding as required and applying stain or finish. Install new glides if they are needed.

In some instances, trimming the bottom of the offending leg(s) would ruin the looks of the piece. In these situations, you may want to build up the leg with a pad until the project is level, then shape the pad to the contour of the leg and finish it to match.

You also can opt for adjustable glides screwed in with T-nuts, as on appliances. If all else fails, head back to the workbench to fashion a replacement leg.

PINT-SIZE PICTURE FRAME

Here's a terrific way to showcase a favorite photograph. And our special routing jig makes it easy for you to mass-produce frame after frame after frame for family or friends.

Note: You'll need 7/16" and 3/16" stock for this project. You can either plane or resaw thicker lumber to this thickness.

Start with the routing jig

1. Cut a piece of 1/2"- or 3/4"-thick stock (we used walnut) to 4 1/4 × 5 1/4". With carbon paper or by adhering a photocopy, transfer the Full-Sized Oval Pattern, page 20, to the center of the stock.

2. Drill a blade-start hole, and carefully cut and sand the opening to shape. (We cut the oval with a *continued*

PINT-SIZE PICTURE FRAME
continued

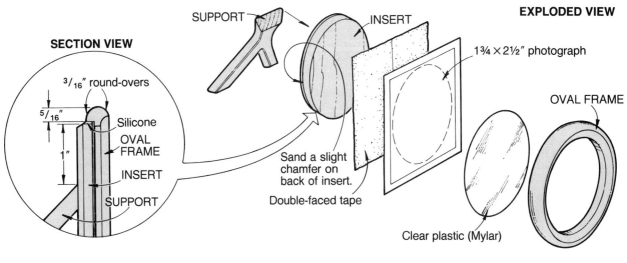

SECTION VIEW

3/16" round-overs

5/16"

Silicone

OVAL FRAME

1"

INSERT

SUPPORT

SUPPORT

INSERT

Sand a slight chamfer on back of insert.

Double-faced tape

EXPLODED VIEW

1¾ × 2½" photograph

OVAL FRAME

Clear plastic (Mylar)

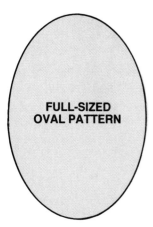

FULL-SIZED OVAL PATTERN

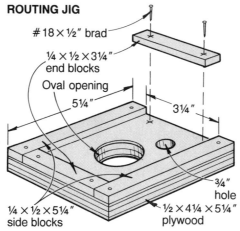

ROUTING JIG

#18 × ½" brad

¼ × ½ × 3¼"
end blocks

Oval opening

5¼"

3¼"

¾"
hole

¼ × ½ × 5¼"
side blocks

½ × 4¼ × 5¼"
plywood

scrollsaw and sanded the opening smooth with a 1" drum sander.)

3. Construct the jig shown on the Routing Jig Drawing, *above, center.* Drill a ¾" hole through a corner of the jig.

Cut and rout the oval to shape

1. Cut a piece of ⁷⁄₁₆" stock to 3¼ × 4¼" for each frame desired. (We planed a 3¼"-wide by 18"-long piece of ½" walnut to ⁷⁄₁₆" thick. Then we crosscut four 4¼"-long blanks from the length.) Check for a snug fit of the frame blank in the routing jig opening.

2. Fit a frame blank into the jig. Bore a ⅝" hole through its center.

3. Mount a ⅝" flush-trimming bit with a ⅝" pilot bearing to your table-mounted router. Position the jig and bit where shown on Step 1 of the Routing the Oval Frame to Shape Drawing, *opposite.* See the Buying Guide for our source of bits.

4. Start the router and run the bearing along the inside edge of the jig to rout the oval interior.

5. Switch to a ½" pilot bearing on the router bit, lower the bit to the level shown on Step 2 of the drawing, and rout a ⅛"-deep rabbet along the bottom of the walnut blank.

6. Stick a dowel through the ¾" hole in the jig to push the blank free. Follow Step 3 on the

drawing to finish routing the interior with an ogee bit.

7. Set the pencil in a compass ⁵⁄₁₆" from the point. As shown in photo A, *below,* stick the compass point *in the rabbet,* and mark the oval exterior onto the blank. Cut the exterior of the frame to shape.

8. Using a ³⁄₁₆" round-over bit and referring to Step 4 on the drawing, rout round-overs on the outside edges of the oval frame.

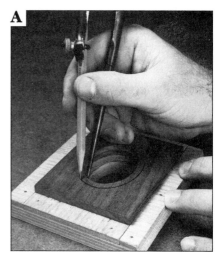

A

With a ⁵⁄₁₆" gap between the lead and point of the compass, mark the oval perimeter on the frame.

ROUTING THE OVAL FRAME TO SHAPE

STEP 1

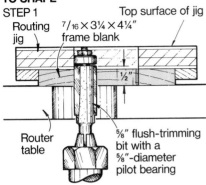

Routing jig

Top surface of jig

$7/16 \times 3\frac{1}{4} \times 4\frac{1}{4}$" frame blank

$\frac{1}{2}$"

Router table

$\frac{5}{8}$" flush-trimming bit with a $\frac{5}{8}$"-diameter pilot bearing

STEP 2

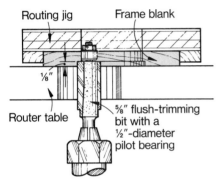

Routing jig

Frame blank

$\frac{1}{8}$"

Router table

$\frac{5}{8}$" flush-trimming bit with a $\frac{1}{2}$"-diameter pilot bearing

STEP 3

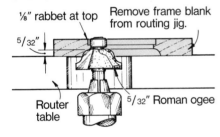

$\frac{1}{8}$" rabbet at top

Remove frame blank from routing jig.

$5/32$"

Router table

$5/32$" Roman ogee

STEP 4

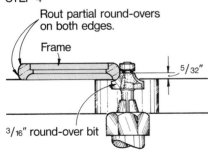

Rout partial round-overs on both edges.

Frame

$5/32$"

$3/16$" round-over bit

Make the insert

1. Lay the frame, rabbet side down, on a piece of $\frac{3}{16}$"-thick stock. Hold a sharpened pencil at an angle, and trace the rabbeted opening's shape onto the $\frac{3}{16}$" stock for the insert. Cut the insert to rough shape, cutting slightly outside the marked line. Sand to the marked line, and check the fit of the insert in the rabbeted opening in the oval frame. (We left about $\frac{1}{32}$" gap between the frame and insert.)

2. Sand a chamfer along the back edge of the insert where shown on the Exploded View Drawing, *opposite, top.*

3. Using the insert as a template, cut a piece of clear plastic (we used a Mylar page protector available at office-supply stores). Utilize the oval plastic insert as a template to cut the photo to shape.

Shape the frame support

1. Transfer the front view from the Full-Sized Support Pattern, *below,* to $\frac{3}{16}$" stock. Cut the support to shape. Sand bevels on the support ends where shown on the Side View. (As an option, delete the support, and epoxy a magnet to the frame back. This lets you display your photos on a refrigerator.)

2. Locate and glue the support to the back side of the insert.

FULL-SIZED SUPPORT PATTERN

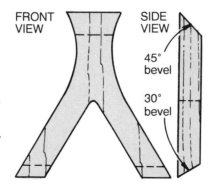

FRONT VIEW

SIDE VIEW

45° bevel

30° bevel

---

3. Sand smooth, and apply finish to the frame, insert, and rear support.

Assemble the frame

1. Adhere the photo to the front of the insert with double-faced tape.

2. Slip the clear plastic into the back of the frame. Center the insert in the rabbeted opening and temporarily hold it in place with masking tape. As shown in photo B, *below,* apply silicone to hold the insert in place. Wipe off excess sealant. If you wish to change the picture later, use a hobby knife to slice through the pliable silicone.

B

Apply silicone sealant between the frame and insert; wipe off excess.

Supplies: #18 × $\frac{1}{2}$" brads, silicone sealant, double-faced tape, clear plastic (DuPont Mylar) page protector, finish.

Buying Guide

• **Carbide-tipped router bits.** $\frac{5}{8}$" flush-trimming bit with $\frac{5}{8}$" bearing, catalog no. C1081; $\frac{1}{2}$" replacement bearing (used to cut the rabbet), catalog no. C3081; $\frac{5}{32}$" Roman ogee, catalog no. C1153; $\frac{3}{16}$" round-over bit, catalog no. C1176. For current prices, contact Cascade Tool Inc., P.O. Box 3110, Bellingham, WA 98227. Or call 800-235-0272.

STACKED-MOLDING PICTURE FRAME

F inding run-of-the-mill picture frames never seems to be a problem. But, if you want a truly unique frame that you can build yourself and size to meet your framing requirements, then we've got just the project for you.

Note: We machined each molding for our 25×33" frame from one long length (we used 12' stock). But you might find it easier to handle two shorter lengths instead. Either way, cut a piece of mahogany about 10" long and use it as a test piece before machining the long length.

To determine the total length of each molding needed, simply measure the perimeter (the total of the four sides) of the item you plan to frame; then add 24" to that figure to allow for miter cuts and waste. The Molding Length Chart, bottom right, lists the figures for several common mat and print sizes.

Shape the mahogany molding

1. Rip enough 1⅜"-thick mahogany (we planed down 1½" stock) to 1¾" wide for the outer frame parts (A). Crosscut to the length needed. (Refer to the note *above* and the Molding Length Chart, *right,* for help with this.)

2. Using carbon paper or a photocopy machine, transfer the full-sized pattern of part A (see the Assembled Frame Detail, *opposite*) to white paper or tablet-type cardboard. Cut the template to shape, and trace the profile onto both ends of the mahogany.

Note: Study the molding drawings carefully because you'll need to turn the mahogany several times when making the dado and router cuts. To help

ensure that we started the cuts on the correct end, we marked an A on one end and a B on the opposite end.

3. Fasten a ½"-wide dado blade and an auxiliary wood fence to your tablesaw. Now raise the dado blade ⁹⁄₁₆" above the surface of the saw table. Using the setup shown on the Step 1 Drawing on page 24 and a pushstick for safety, cut a ⅜" rabbet ⁹⁄₁₆" deep along one edge of the test strip. Check the cut against the marked profile; then make the cut along the mahogany piece starting at the end labeled A. Reposition the

Molding Length Chart	
Common Mat and Print Sizes	Total Length of Molding Needed
8 × 10"	60"
11 × 14"	74"
12 × 16"	80"
16 × 20"	96"
18 × 24"	108"
20 × 24"	112"

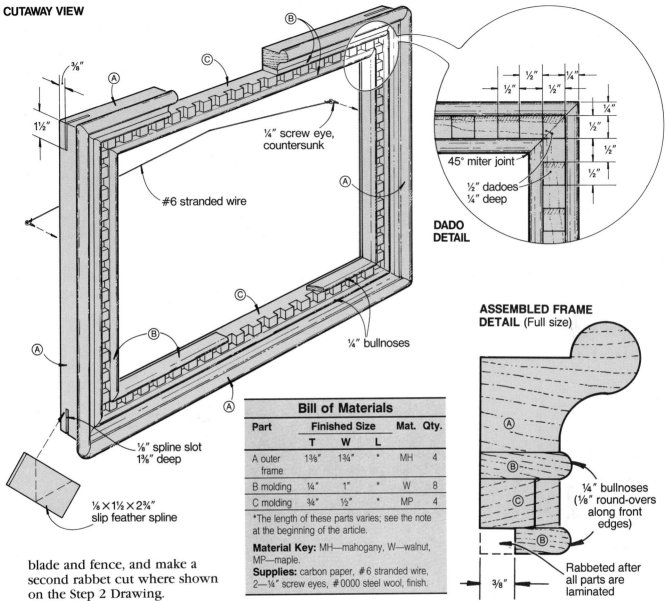

3/8"

1½"

Ⓐ

Ⓒ

Ⓑ

¼" screw eye,
countersunk

#6 stranded wire

Ⓐ

Ⓒ

Ⓑ

¼" bullnoses

Ⓐ

Ⓐ

⅛" spline slot
1⅜" deep

⅛ × 1½ × 2¾"
slip feather spline

**DADO
DETAIL**

½" ½" ¼"

½" ½"

¼"

½"

½"

½"

45° miter joint

½" dadoes
¼" deep

**ASSEMBLED FRAME
DETAIL** (Full size)

Ⓐ

Ⓑ

Ⓒ

Ⓑ

¼" bullnoses
(⅛" round-overs
along front
edges)

Rabbeted after
all parts are
laminated

3/8"

Bill of Materials

Part	Finished Size			Mat.	Qty.
	T	**W**	**L**		
A outer frame	1⅜"	1¾"	*	MH	4
B molding	¼"	1"	*	W	8
C molding	¾"	½"	*	MP	4

*The length of these parts varies; see the note at the beginning of the article.

Material Key: MH—mahogany, W—walnut, MP—maple.
Supplies: carbon paper, #6 stranded wire, 2—¼" screw eyes, #0000 steel wool, finish.

blade and fence, and make a second rabbet cut where shown on the Step 2 Drawing.

4. Reposition the rip fence again, raise the dado blade, turn the mahogany end for end, and remove the excess material where shown on the Step 3 Drawing.

5. Cut a ¼ × ⁷⁄₁₆" support block the same length as the router table. Using double-faced tape, adhere the support block to the router table where shown on the Step 4 Drawing. The support block prevents the mahogany piece from falling onto the router bit and ruining the molding. Next, chuck a ⅜" bead/quarter-round bit (without the ball-bearing pilot) to a table-mounted router (see the Buying Guide,

page 25, for our source of router bits). With the end labeled A next to the bit, start the router, slowly push the mahogany stock into the bit, and rout a round-over along the inside edge of the molding where shown on the Step 4 Drawing.

6. Relocate the support block on the router table, and reposition the router fence. Turn the stock end for end so the end labeled B faces the bit, and round over the opposite edge of the mahogany stock where shown on the Step 5 Drawing.

7. Remove the support block from the router table. Using the Step 6 Drawing for reference, turn the stock end for end, and round over the remainder of the outside edge.

8. Switch to a ½" cove bit (without the ball-bearing pilot), reposition the router table fence, and make several routing passes, raising the bit each pass until you reach a ⅝" height, to cove the area shown on the Step 7 Drawing. *continued*

STACKED-MOLDING PICTURE FRAME
continued

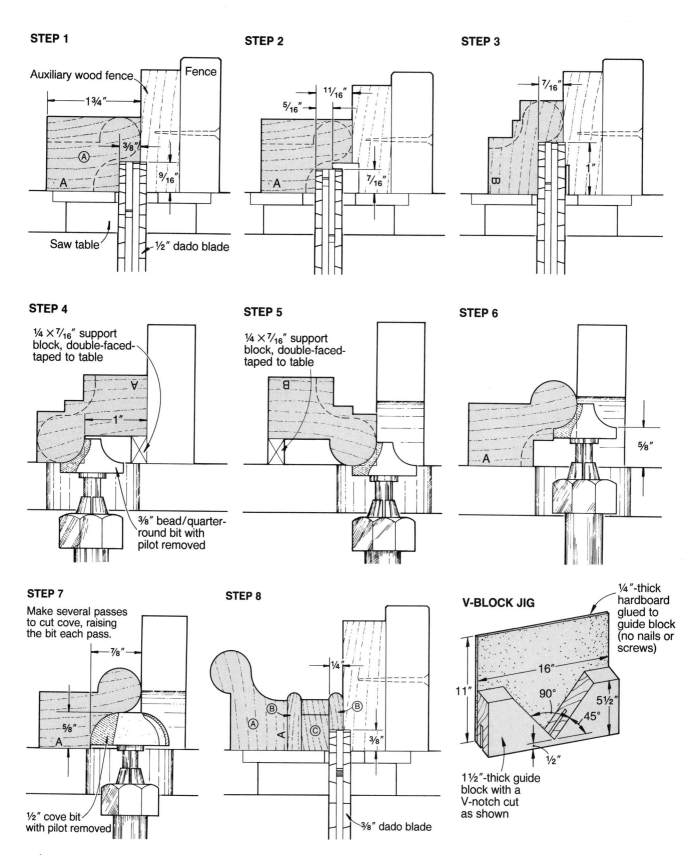

STEP 1

Auxiliary wood fence
Fence
1¾"
Ⓐ
⅜"
A
9/16"
Saw table
½" dado blade

STEP 2

11/16"
5/16"
A
7/16"

STEP 3

7/16"
B
1"

STEP 4

¼ × 7/16" support block, double-faced-taped to table
A
1"
⅜" bead/quarter-round bit with pilot removed

STEP 5

¼ × 7/16" support block, double-faced-taped to table
B

STEP 6

A
⅝"

STEP 7

Make several passes to cut cove, raising the bit each pass.
⅞"
⅝"
A
½" cove bit with pilot removed

STEP 8

¼"
Ⓑ
Ⓐ A Ⓒ Ⓑ
⅜"
⅜" dado blade

V-BLOCK JIG

¼"-thick hardboard glued to guide block (no nails or screws)
16"
11"
90°
5½"
45°
½"
1½"-thick guide block with a V-notch cut as shown

Form the walnut molding

1. Resaw enough 1¹⁄₁₆" walnut for the ¼"-thick molding (B). You'll need two strips the same length as the mahogany molding. Rip the walnut to 1" wide, and crosscut the strips to the same length as the mahogany molding.

2. Chuck a ⅛" round-over bit (see the Buying Guide for our source) into the collet of your table-mounted router, and rout a round-over on the top and bottom of one edge of each strip to create a bullnose. Sand the molding smooth.

Form the maple molding

1. To form the dadoed molding (C), start by ripping a piece of ¾"-thick maple to ½" wide. Crosscut it to the same length as the other moldings.

2. Lay out lines ½" apart the entire length of the maple strip. Attach a ½" dado blade to your radial-arm saw, and cut the ¼"-deep dadoes as shown in photo A, *below*. (We replaced the fence on our radial-arm saw with a new one, and then cut through it with the dado blade. The ½"-wide kerf in the new fence makes it easy to accurately line up the dado lines with the blade and also prevents chip-out.) After cutting all the dadoes, sand the strip smooth.

A

Align the dado lines you marked on the maple with the dado cut in the fence.

Assemble the frame

1. Glue and clamp one of the walnut strips (B) to the mahogany (A), with the *back* edges flush (see the Assembled Frame Detail accompanying the Cutaway View Drawing, page 23). Allow the glue to dry. (We used wood spacers between the clamp head and moldings to prevent marring of the wood.) Later, glue and clamp the maple strip (C) to the walnut-mahogany lamination, with the *back* edges flush. (Use a sharp chisel to scrape away the excess glue from the dadoes before it dries. We found it much harder to keep from scratching the wood after the glue had dried.) Glue and clamp the remaining walnut strip (B) to the maple strip, with its *back* flush with that of the rest of the lamination.

2. Attach a ⅜" dado blade to your tablesaw arbor. With the end labeled B facing the blade, start the saw, and cut a ¼" rabbet ⅜" deep along the back edge of the frame lamination where shown on the Step 8 Drawing.

3. Miter-cut the frame lamination to the lengths needed for the four frame sides. For perfectly matched corners when making the mitered cuts, cut at the corner of a maple square or dadoed gap where shown on the Dado Detail, page 23.

4. Checking for square, glue and clamp the four frame sides together. (We used a band clamp for this.)

5. Using a V-block jig (see the V-Block Jig Drawing, *opposite, bottom right,* if you don't have one), cut a ⅛" spline slot 1⅜" deep in each corner of the assembled frame as shown in photo B, *top right.*

6. Cut four feather splines (we resawed walnut) to the size stated on the Cutaway View Drawing. Glue the walnut feather splines in the spline slots you just cut in each corner. Later, after the glue has dried, trim and sand the splines flush with the mahogany.

B

Use a V-block jig to cut the spline slot in each frame corner.

Apply the finish

1. Apply two coats of sanding sealer, steel-wooling between coats. Be sure to remove all the steel wool, especially from between the dadoes, before applying the next coat. (We used a vacuum cleaner with a brush attachment to clean the residual steel wool from the frame after each rubdown with steel wool.)

2. Apply two coats of finish (we used lacquer), again steel-wooling between coats. Mount your artwork.

3. To hang the frame, countersink two holes on the back side of the frame where shown on the Cutaway View Drawing (countersinking helps the frame hang flatter against the wall). Now turn ¼" screw eyes into each countersink. String #6 stranded wire from screw eye to screw eye. Hang.

Buying Guide

• **⅛" round-over bit.** Catalog no. C1175. Contact Cascade Tool Inc., P.O. Box 3110, Bellingham, WA 98227. Or call 800-235-0272.

• **Router bits and arbor set.** ⅜" bead/quarter-round bit, catalog no. 9HT25562; ½" cove bit, catalog no. 9HT2557. Arbor set to be used with the bead/quarter-round and cove bits, catalog no. 9HT25601. Bits and arbor set available at Sears.

TABLETOP EASEL

Wₑ'll bet you never see an easel this attractive in any gift shop. Jim Boelling, our project builder, built the original easel to display pictures of his children. With just a few pieces of wood and a few hours in the shop, you can support your own photos, needlework, or artwork.

Cut the legs and spreader

1. From ¾"-thick walnut, cut two strips ¾" wide by 15" long for the front legs (A), one strip ¾×11" for the rear leg (B), and a fourth strip ¾×8" for the spreader (C). The pieces are cut slightly long for safety in machining.

2. Build a jig from ¾" stock (we used plywood) to the shape shown on the Jig Pattern, *opposite, bottom center.* Follow Step 1 of the Cutting the Front Legs Drawing, *below,* to angle-cut the *top* end of both legs. Tilt the saw blade, angle the miter gauge, and cut the compound angle on the *bottom* of both *front* legs as shown on steps 2 and 3.

continued

CUTTING THE FRONT LEGS

STEP 1

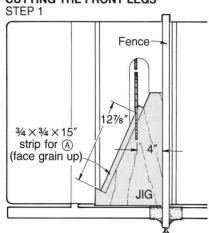

Fence

¾ × ¾ × 15"
strip for Ⓐ
(face grain up)

12⅞"

4"

JIG

STEP 2   LEFT LEG

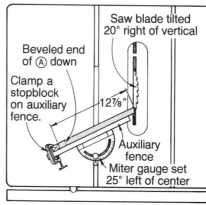

Saw blade tilted
20° right of vertical

Beveled end
of Ⓐ down

Clamp a
stopblock
on auxiliary
fence.

12⅞"

Auxiliary
fence

Miter gauge set
25° left of center

STEP 3   RIGHT LEG

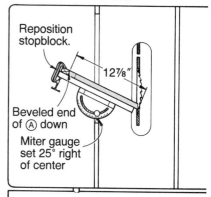

Reposition
stopblock.

12⅞"

Beveled end
of Ⓐ down

Miter gauge
set 25° right
of center

EXPLODED VIEW

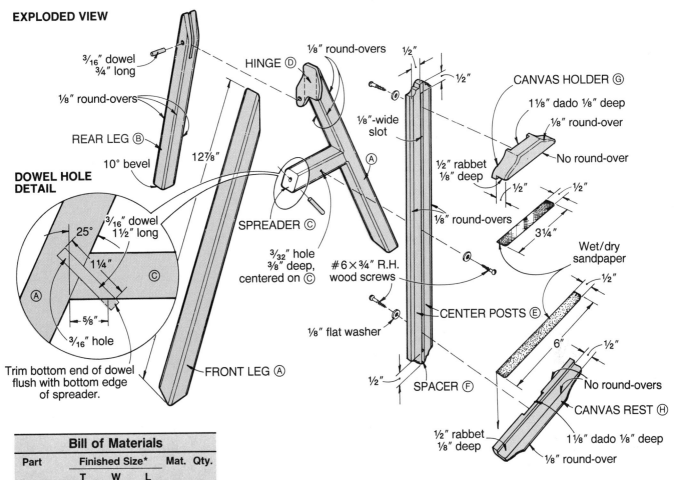

3/16" dowel 3/4" long

1/8" round-overs

REAR LEG Ⓑ

10° bevel

DOWEL HOLE DETAIL

25°

3/16" dowel 1 1/2" long

1 1/4"

Ⓐ

Ⓒ

5/8"

3/16" hole

Trim bottom end of dowel flush with bottom edge of spreader.

HINGE Ⓓ

1/8" round-overs

1/2"

1/8"-wide slot

Ⓐ

SPREADER Ⓒ

3/32" hole 3/8" deep, centered on Ⓒ

#6 × 3/4" R.H. wood screws

1/8" flat washer

FRONT LEG Ⓐ

1/2"

1/2"

1/2" rabbet 1/8" deep

1/8" round-overs

CENTER POSTS Ⓔ

1/2"

SPACER Ⓕ

1/2" rabbet 1/8" deep

CANVAS HOLDER Ⓖ

1 1/8" dado 1/8" deep

1/8" round-over

No round-over

1/2"

1/2"

3 1/4"

Wet/dry sandpaper

1/2"

6"

1/2"

No round-overs

CANVAS REST Ⓗ

1 1/8" dado 1/8" deep

1/8" round-over

Bill of Materials

Part	Finished Size*			Mat.	Qty.
	T	W	L		
A* front leg	3/4"	3/4"	12 7/8"	W	2
B* rear leg	5/8"	3/4"	10 1/4"	W	1
C* spreader	3/4"	3/4"	3 5/8"	W	1
D* hinge	1/8"	1 1/2"	2 3/8"	WV	5
E center post	3/8"	1/2"	14"	W:	2
F spacer	1/8"	3/8"	1/2"	W	2
G* canvas holder	3/4"	3/4"	3 1/4"	W	1
H* canvas rest	3/4"	3/4"	6"	W	1

*Parts marked with an * are cut larger initially, then trimmed to finished size. Please read the instructions before cutting.

Material Key: W—walnut, WV—walnut veneer.
Supplies: spray adhesive, 3—#6×3/4" roundhead brass wood screws with 1/8" brass flat washers, 3/16" dowel, wet/dry sandpaper, double-faced tape, finish, #0000 steel wool.

Cutting Diagram
3/4 × 4 × 36" Walnut
*Note: Resaw Ⓔ and Ⓕ from the 3/4" stock.

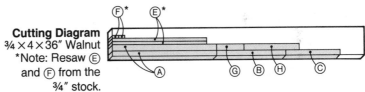

Ⓕ* Ⓔ*

Ⓐ Ⓖ Ⓑ Ⓗ Ⓒ

JIG PATTERN

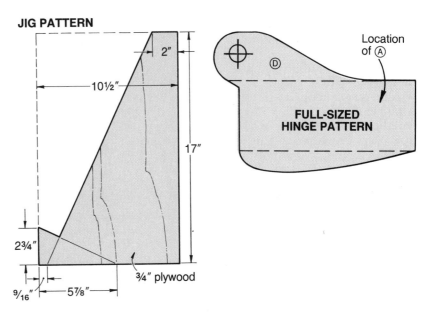

2"

10 1/2"

17"

2 3/4"

3/4" plywood

9/16"

5 7/8"

Location of Ⓐ

Ⓓ

FULL-SIZED HINGE PATTERN

TABLETOP EASEL
continued

FULL-SIZED PATTERNS

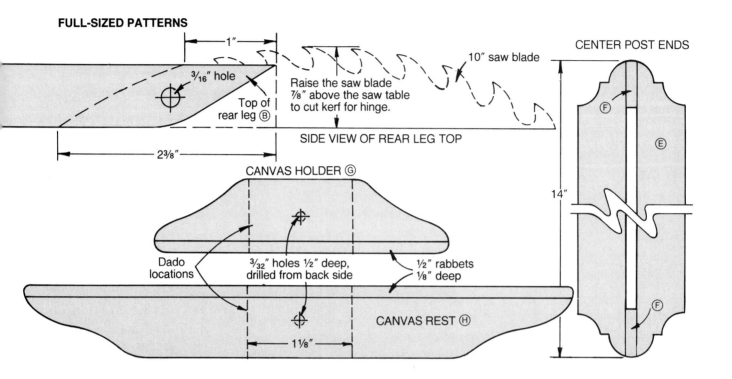

CENTER POST ENDS

1"

3/16" hole

Top of rear leg Ⓑ

2 3/8"

Raise the saw blade 7/8" above the saw table to cut kerf for hinge.

10" saw blade

SIDE VIEW OF REAR LEG TOP

CANVAS HOLDER Ⓖ

Dado locations

3/32" holes 1/2" deep, drilled from back side

1/2" rabbets 1/8" deep

CANVAS REST Ⓗ

1 1/8"

14"

Ⓕ

Ⓔ

Ⓕ

Ⓕ

3. Cut the rear leg (B) to 10¼" long, cutting a 10° bevel across the bottom end. Cut the spreader (C) to length (3⅝"), cutting each end at a 25° angle (refer to the Dowel Hole Detail accompanying the Exploded View Drawing, page 27.)

Cut the hinge and join the front legs

1. For a nearly unbreakable hinge (D), cut five pieces of walnut veneer about 3×3" and laminate them together with wood glue. Alternate the grain direction of each piece. This will result in a piece with a finished thickness of ⅛".

2. Using carbon paper or a photocopy and spray adhesive, transfer the Full-Sized Hinge Pattern, page 27, to the ⅛" veneer lamination. With a bandsaw or scrollsaw, cut the hinge (D) to shape. Sand smooth.

With the front legs propped up on six flat washers, glue the hinge piece between the legs.

3. Glue and tape the hinge between the front legs. (As shown in the photo, *opposite,* we clamped a board in our woodworker's vise. After positioning the bottom ends of the front legs against the board, we placed small handscrew clamps on the board to hold the legs in position as we glued and taped the hinge between the leg tops. The six washers shown in the photo were used to hold the top end of the legs off the table, allowing the hinge to protrude.)

4. Glue and tape the spreader (C) between the front legs. After the glue dries, mark a pair of centerpoints on the bottom of the spreader ⅝″ from the joint lines where shown on the Dowel Hole Detail, page 27.

5. To strengthen the joints between the spreader and front legs, secure the front-leg frame in a woodworker's vise. Drill a pair of ³⁄₁₆″ holes through the spreader and into the front legs where shown on the Dowel Hole Detail. (We eyeballed the angles and drilled the holes with a brad-point bit.)

6. Cut two ³⁄₁₆″ dowels 1½″ long. Put a dab of glue in each hole, and tap the dowels into position. Trim the excess dowel flush with the bottom edge of the spreader.

7. Find the center and drill a ³⁄₃₂″ hole ⅜″ deep in the front surface of the spreader (refer to the Exploded View Drawing, page 27).

Make the hinged rear leg

1. To cut the hinge kerf in the rear leg, start by marking a line across the rear leg (B) 1″ from the top end. Next, raise a ⅛″-wide tablesaw blade ⅞″ above the saw table. Position the fence to center the blade on the top end of the rear leg. Start the saw,

and push the rear leg into the blade until the blade reaches the marked line where shown on the Full-Sized Patterns, *opposite.* Carefully back away the rear leg from the blade before turning off the saw.

2. Mark the curve on the kerfed end of the rear leg, and cut the top end of the rear leg to shape. Referring to the Full-Sized Patterns, mark the centerpoint and drill a ³⁄₁₆″ hole through the top end of the rear leg.

3. Sand or rout a ⅛″ round-over on all edges of the front-leg frame (A, C) and rear leg (B).

Assemble the center posts

1. Cut the center posts (E) and spacers (F) to size from ⅜″ stock (we planed a thicker piece down to this size).

2. Now, with the ends and surfaces flush, glue and clamp the spacers between the center posts where shown on the Exploded View Drawing.

3. Transfer the Center Post Ends Pattern, *opposite,* to both ends of the center-post assembly. Cut the ends to shape (we used a scrollsaw for this task).

4. Sand or rout ⅛″ round-overs along outside edges (not the ends) of the center-post assembly.

Add the canvas rest and canvas holder

1. On the tablesaw, cut a piece of ¾″-thick walnut to ¾ × 12″ for the canvas holder (G) and the canvas rest (H).

2. Cut or rout a ½″ rabbet ⅛″ deep the length of the strip.

3. Transfer the full-sized Canvas Rest and Holder patterns, hole centerpoints, and dado locations shown *opposite* to the strip. Cut the 1⅛″ dadoes ⅛″ deep where marked on the back side (the side adjacent the ½″ rabbet). Drill ³⁄₃₂″ holes ½″ deep from the back side (same side as the dadoes), and cut the ends of the pieces to shape.

4. Sand or rout ⅛″ round-overs along the edges of the canvas holder and rest where shown on the Exploded View Drawing.

5. Cut two pieces of wet/dry sandpaper to the sizes shown on the Exploded View Drawing. Using double-faced tape or glue, adhere the pieces to the rabbets in the canvas holder and rest where shown on the drawing. The sandpaper helps prevent artwork from sliding around in the rabbet.

Assemble the easel

1. Mask the sandpaper adhered to the canvas rest and holder, and apply the finish to all parts, rubbing lightly with #0000 steel wool between coats. (We applied an aerosol lacquer, Deft Clear Wood Finish.) After the finish dries, remove the masking tape.

2. Fasten the canvas rest and holder to the center-post assembly with #6 × ¾″ brass wood screws and brass washers. Use the same-size screw to fasten the center-post assembly to the spreader.

3. Tape the rear leg (B) in position against the hinge (D). Using the previously drilled ³⁄₁₆″ hole in the top of the rear leg as a guide, drill a ³⁄₁₆″ hole through the hinge. Cut a ³⁄₁₆″ dowel to ¾″ in length. Stain the ends of the dowel to match the walnut (walnut dowels are not commonly available in ³⁄₁₆″ diameter). With the holes aligned, insert the ³⁄₁₆″ dowel through the holes to act as a hinge pin.

OCCASIONAL TABLES

Three coffee tables, a stately hall table, a curvaceous end table, even a pint-size picnic table—the projects on the following pages can keep you turning out tables for several seasons to come.

CONTEMPORARY COFFEE TABLE

The sleek coffee table shown *opposite* represents one of the best contemporary project designs we've seen in a long while. It's also an opportunity to test your skill at making open mortise-and-tenon joints, as well as dovetails. We selected smoked glass for the tabletop, but you could substitute acrylic or even solid wood.

Build the table legs

1. Rip, then crosscut table parts A, B, and C to the dimensions listed in the Bill of Materials.

2. Lay out a tenon on one end of each part A where shown on the Open Mortise and Tenon Drawing, *below.* Then make the two cuts with a bandsaw fitted with a sharp ⅜″ or ½″ blade. We clamped a stop on the bandsaw fence to ensure a 4″-long cut on all pieces. Now crosscut the remainder with a tablesaw, radial-arm saw, or dovetail saw.

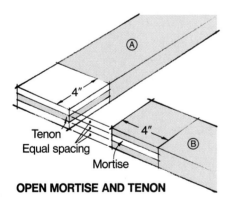

OPEN MORTISE AND TENON

3. Lay out and cut a mortise on both ends of each leg (B) where shown on the drawing *above.* Use the bandsaw and stop as you did for the tenon. Test-fit a tenon into this mortise, then cut the rest of the mortises. Now clean out the mortises with a sharp chisel.

Cutting Diagram

15/16 × 9¼ × 96″ Oak

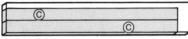

15/16 × 7¼ × 48″ Oak

11/16 × 5½ × 48″ Oak

4. Spread an even coating of glue on the mating surfaces of the mortises and tenons, then clamp each of the legs together with the supports (A). Check for square.

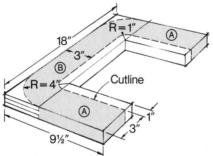

LAYING OUT THE LEG

5. Lay out the final shape of each leg as shown on the Laying Out the Leg Drawing, *above,* then use a bandsaw or jigsaw to cut the legs to their final shape. Sand all surfaces smooth. (We used a drum sander to smooth the inside curves and a belt sander to sand the outside curves.)

6. With a router and a ⅜″ round-over bit, round over all edges *except* those along the top inside of the legs where the smoked glass will fit and the area of the as-yet-uncut dovetail joints (refer to the Dovetail Joint Detail, page 32).

7. Using a router fitted with a ¼″ slotting cutter, cut an 8″-long, ½″-deep stopped groove along

Bill of Materials					
Part	Finished Size			Mat.	Qty.
	T	W	L		
A support	15/16″	4″	9½″	O	8
B leg	15/16″	4″	18″	O	4
C rail	15/16″	3″	45″	O	2
D stretcher	11/16″	2½″	42⅜″	O	2

Material Key: O—oak.
Supplies: 4—¼ × 3″ lag screws with washers, ¼″ hardboard for splines, ½″-diameter oak dowel, 1″-diameter oak dowel, finish of your choice, ⅜″ smoked glass or acrylic.

the inside edge of each leg. (Center the groove top to bottom and side to side, as shown on the End View Drawing, page 32.) If you don't have a slotting cutter, cut the groove on a router table fitted with a fence and a straight bit. You could also join the legs with dowels.

8. Using ¼″ hardboard, cut four ⅞″-wide splines 8″ long. Shape both ends of each spline to fit the groove. Then insert (but do not glue) the splines between the legs. The splines should fit snugly without creating a gap between the legs.

9. Working on a flat surface, glue and clamp both leg assemblies together, checking that the bottoms and tops are flush and that the surfaces remain level. When the glue dries, lay out the location of the *continued*

CONTEMPORARY COFFEE TABLE
continued

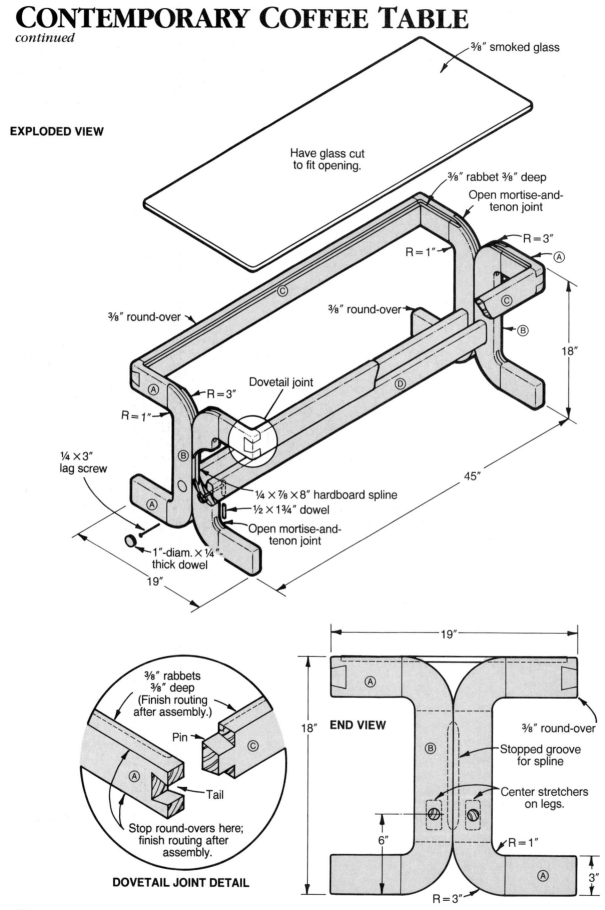

EXPLODED VIEW

⅜" smoked glass

Have glass cut
to fit opening.

⅜" rabbet ⅜" deep

Open mortise-and-
tenon joint

R = 1"

R = 3"

Ⓐ

Ⓒ

Ⓒ

Ⓑ

18"

⅜" round-over

⅜" round-over

Dovetail joint

Ⓓ

Ⓐ

R = 3"

R = 1"

¼ × 3"
lag screw

Ⓑ

¼ × ⅞ × 8" hardboard spline

½ × 1¾" dowel

Open mortise-and-
tenon joint

Ⓐ

45"

1"-diam. × ¼"-
thick dowel

19"

DOVETAIL JOINT DETAIL

⅜" rabbets
⅜" deep
(Finish routing
after assembly.)

Pin

Ⓒ

Ⓐ

Tail

Stop round-overs here;
finish routing after
assembly.

END VIEW

19"

Ⓐ

18"

Ⓑ

⅜" round-over

Stopped groove
for spline

Center stretchers
on legs.

6"

R = 1"

R = 3"

3"

Ⓐ

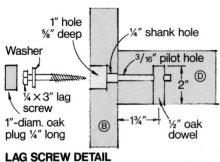

1" hole
⅝" deep
Washer
¼ shank hole
³⁄₁₆" pilot hole
Ⓓ
2"
¼ × 3" lag screw
1"-diam. oak plug ¼" long
Ⓑ
←1¾"→
½" oak dowel

LAG SCREW DETAIL

lag-screw joint on both legs; see the End View Drawing, *opposite, bottom right,* for positioning information. Drill a 1" hole ⅝" deep at each point, then drill a ¼" hole in the center of the 1" hole through the stock as shown on the Lag Screw Detail, *above.* Prevent tear-out of the grain on the back side of the legs by backing them with scrap stock when drilling.

Make the dovetails

1. Lay out a pin at each end of each rail (C) as shown on the Laying Out the Pin Drawing, *below,* then make the cuts in the sequence indicated using a dovetail saw.

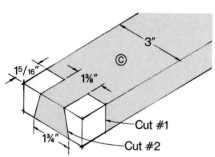

3"
1⁵⁄₁₆"
1⅜"
Ⓒ
1¾"
Cut #1
Cut #2

LAYING OUT THE PIN

2. Lay out the leg assemblies (A–B) on a flat surface and use a crafts knife to scribe the outline of the tails onto the ends of the top A parts as shown on the Scribing the Tail Drawing, *center right.*

Cut a tail on one end of A with a dovetail saw. Clamp a piece of wood squarely across the top of the tail and use it to guide your chisel to clean out the remainder as shown in the photo, *top right.* After cutting the first tail, check

that the pins on the ends of C fit snugly into it, then cut the rest of the tails.

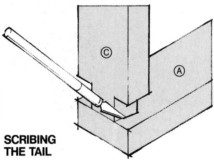

Ⓒ
Ⓐ

SCRIBING THE TAIL

Assemble and finish the table

1. Rip, then crosscut the stretchers (D) to size. Measure in from each end of each stretcher and drill a ½" hole 2" deep as shown on the Lag Screw Detail, *top left.*

2. Glue, then insert a ½" oak dowel 2" long into each of the holes. (This whole process ensures a stronger joint between the legs and stretchers when the leg assembly is screwed in place later.) After the glue dries, sand the dowels flush.

3. Glue and clamp the rails (C) and stretchers (D) between the leg assemblies (A–B) as dimensioned on the End View

Drawing. When the glue forms a tough skin, remove the excess.

4. Drill ³⁄₁₆" pilot holes centered in the previously drilled holes in the leg assembly and through the ½" dowel in the stretcher. The hole will house the ¼ × 3" lag screw, as indicated on the Lag Screw Detail. Drive the lag screws through the leg assemblies and into the stretchers and oak dowels.

5. From 1"-diameter oak dowel, cut four ¼"-long plugs (cut the plugs a hair on the long side), then glue and insert them into position to conceal the screws. Sand off the excess plug.

6. Rout a ⅜" rabbet ⅜" deep along the top inside edge of the legs and rails for the glass tabletop. Round over all remaining edges with a ⅜" round-over bit.

7. Finish-sand all surfaces, then apply the finish of your choice. (We used a natural oil finish covered with several coats of finishing wax.)

8. Take your project to a glass supplier and have the personnel there measure for the tabletop and cut it to size. This leaves less room for error.

TRADITIONAL-STYLE HALL TABLE

Simply stated lines and quality cherry lumber make this piece a pleasure to build and a joy to own.

Construct the table's base

1. Rip, then crosscut the 1¾"-thick cherry stock to size for the table legs (A). (If you can't find stock this thick, laminate thinner cherry pieces, then rip and crosscut to size.)

2. Rip the side aprons (B) and the back apron (C) to width and crosscut them to length. Now cut the rails (D) and stiles (E, F) to size for the front frame.

Clamp the frame members (D, E, F) together and mark a pair of dowel holes at each joint. (Mark the joints A–A, B–B, and so on, as shown on the Leg-Rail Doweling Drawing, *below,* so you won't have a problem getting the mating members back together again.) Remove the clamps, then drill ⅜" dowel holes 13⁄16" deep in pieces D, E, and F. Glue and clamp the front frame (D, E, F) together. Remove glue squeeze-out when the glue forms a tough skin. After the glue dries, sand the assembly smooth.

LEG-RAIL DOWELING

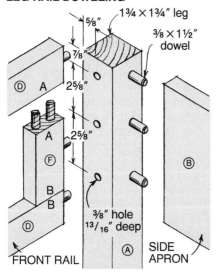

1¾ × 1¾" leg
5⁄8"
7⁄8"
⅜ × 1½" dowel
D   A
2⅝"
A
F
2⅝"
B
B
B
D
⅜" hole 13⁄16" deep
A   SIDE APRON
FRONT RAIL

3. Now clamp the front frame and the side and back aprons (B, C) to the legs. Make marks for dowel holes at each joint. (See the Leg-Rail Doweling Drawing for correct position.) Drill the dowel holes, then glue and clamp the pieces together. Check for square with a framing square. Set the frame upright and check to see that the table stands flat. If it doesn't, adjust the length of the legs as explained on page 18.

Remove excess glue and sand all surfaces.

4. Cut the drawer-guide supports (G), drawer guides (H, I), and kickers (J) to size. Cut a ⅝" rabbet ½" deep along one edge of each side guide (H) and along both edges of the center guide (I). Refer to the Side Drawer Guide and Center Drawer Guide drawings, page 37.

5. With the table base standing upright, dry-clamp the drawer-guide supports (G) *continued*

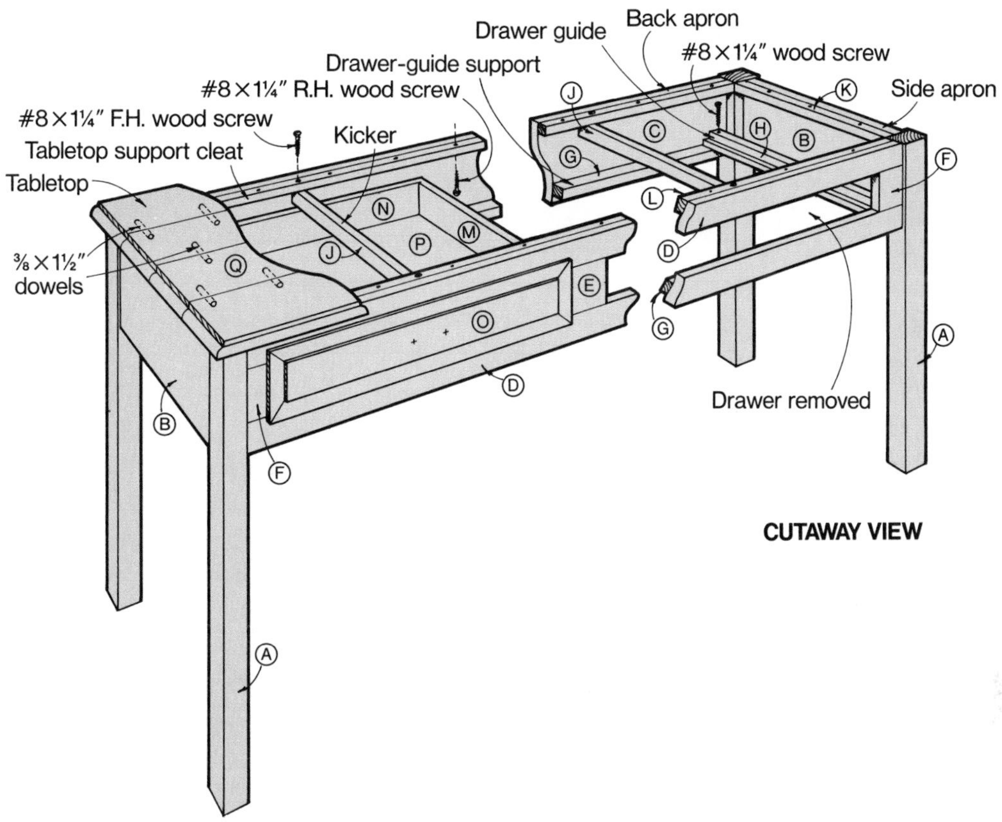
Drawer guide
Back apron
#8×1¼″ wood screw
Drawer-guide support
#8×1¼″ R.H. wood screw
Side apron
#8×1¼″ F.H. wood screw
Kicker
Tabletop support cleat
Tabletop
⅜×1½″ dowels
Drawer removed

CUTAWAY VIEW

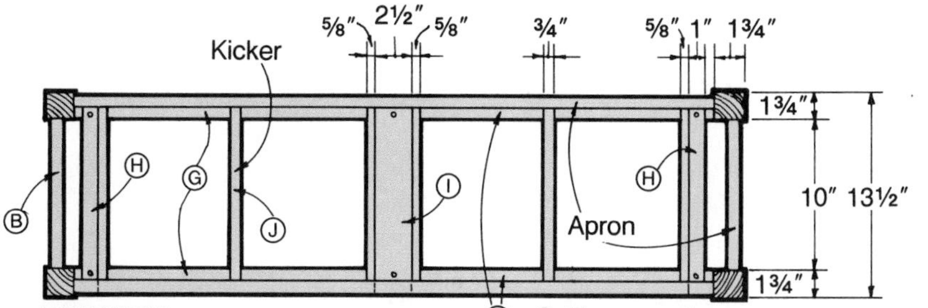
Kicker
⅝″ 2½″ ⅝″
¾″
⅝″ 1″ 1¾″
1¾″
10″ 13½″
1¾″
Apron
Guide supports

TOP VIEW
(Without top and top mounting cleats)

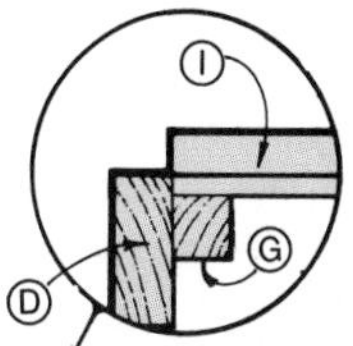

DETAIL
Note: Top of rabbeted edge Ⓘ is flush with top of rail Ⓓ.

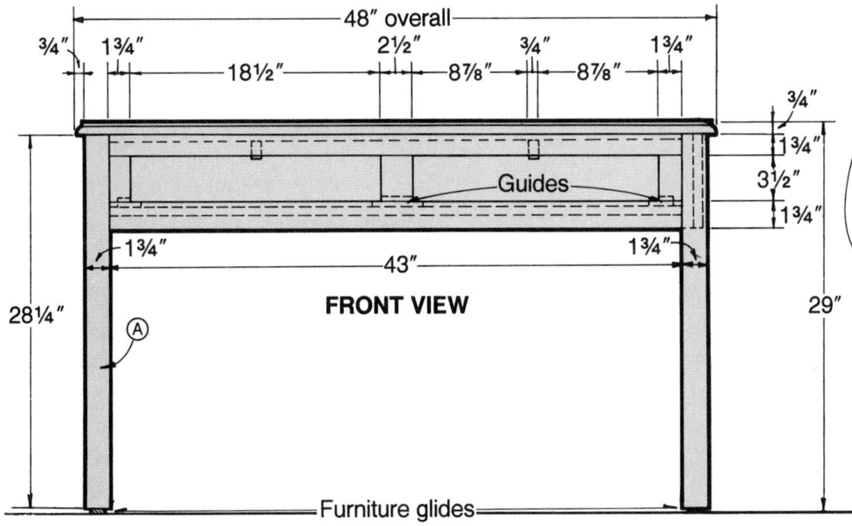
48″ overall
¾″ 1¾″ 18½″ 2½″ 8⅞″ ¾″ 8⅞″ 1¾″
¾″
1¾″
3½″
1¾″
Guides
1¾″ 43″ 1¾″
28¼″
29″
Furniture glides

FRONT VIEW

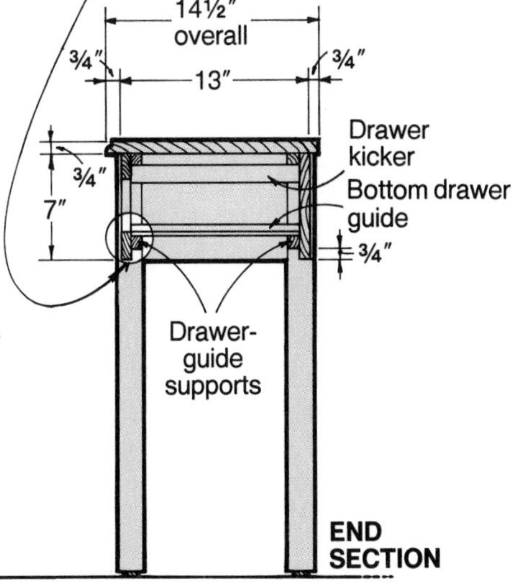
14½″ overall
¾″ 13″ ¾″
¾″
7″
Drawer kicker
Bottom drawer guide
¾″
Drawer-guide supports

END SECTION

TRADITIONAL-STYLE HALL TABLE
continued

Bill of Materials

Part	Finished Size* T	W	L	Mat.	Qty.
A leg	1¾"	1¾"	28¼"	C	4
B side apron	¾"	7"	10"	C	2
C back apron	¾"	7"	43"	C	1
D rail	¾"	1¾"	43"	C	2
E stile	¾"	2½"	3½"	C	1
F stile	¾"	1¾"	3½"	C	2
G guide support	¾"	¾"	43"	C	2
H drawer guide	¾"	1⅝"	11½"	C	2
I drawer guide	¾"	3¾"	11½"	C	1
J kicker	¾"	1³⁄₁₆"	11½"	C	2
K cleat	¾"	¾"	10"	C	2
L cleat	¾"	¾"	43"	C	2
M drawer side	½"	3¼"	12"	C	4
N drawer back	½"	3¼"	17⅞"	C	2
O drawer front	¾"	4¼"	19⅜"	C	2
P drawer bottom	¼"	11½"	17⅞"	CP	2
Q* top	¾"	3⅝"	48"	C	4

*Part marked with an * is cut larger initially, then trimmed to finished size. Please read instructions before cutting.

Material Key: C—cherry, CP—cherry plywood.

Supplies: 2—drawer pulls, #8 × 1¼" roundhead wood screws, ⅜" × 1½" dowels, #8 × 1¼" flathead wood screws, 4—furniture glides.

Cutting Diagram

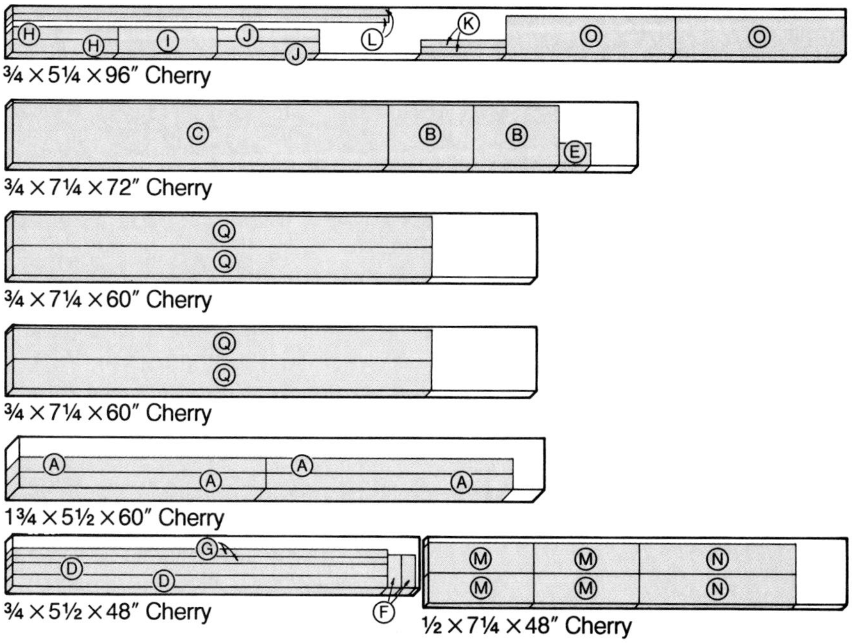
H
H
I
J
J
L
K
O
O
¾ × 5¼ × 96" Cherry
C
B
B
E
¾ × 7¼ × 72" Cherry
Q
Q
¾ × 7¼ × 60" Cherry
Q
Q
¾ × 7¼ × 60" Cherry
A
A
A
A
1¾ × 5½ × 60" Cherry
G
D
D
F
¾ × 5½ × 48" Cherry
M
M
N
M
M
N
½ × 7¼ × 48" Cherry

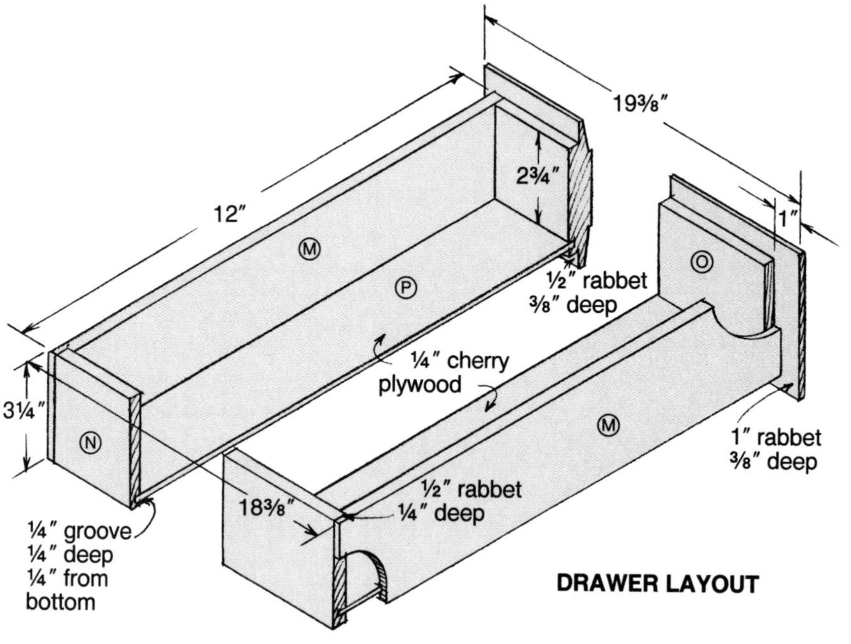
19⅜"
12"
2¾"
1"
M
P
O
½" rabbet
⅜" deep
¼" cherry
plywood
3¼"
N
M
1" rabbet
⅜" deep
½" rabbet
¼" deep
18⅜"
¼" groove
¼" deep
¼" from
bottom
DRAWER LAYOUT

¾" above the bottom of the back apron (C) and the front lower rail (D). To check for correct position of the drawer-guide supports (G), set the drawer guides (H, I) across the top of the supports. The top of the rabbeted portions of H and I should be flush with the top of the bottom rail (D) as shown on the End Section Detail, page 35. Mark the positions of the supports (G); glue and clamp them in place.

6. Cut tabletop support cleats (K, L) to size. Glue and screw them to the base as shown on the Cutaway View Drawing, page 35, flush with the top of the base. Center the kickers (J) in the drawer openings. Screw them to the top-support cleats. Drill ⁵⁄₃₂" pilot holes through K and L for mounting the tabletop.

Make and fit the drawers

1. Start by ripping, then crosscutting the drawer sides (M), backs (N), fronts (O), and bottoms (P) to size.

2. Cut a ¼" groove ¼" deep and ¼" from the bottom of pieces

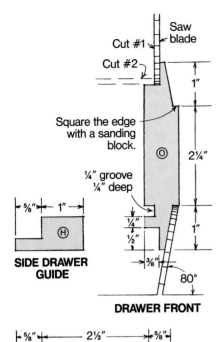

Cut #1 — Saw blade

Cut #2

1"

Square the edge with a sanding block.

2¼"

¼" groove ¼" deep

⅝" — 1"

H

SIDE DRAWER GUIDE

¼"
½"
1"

⅜"

80°

DRAWER FRONT

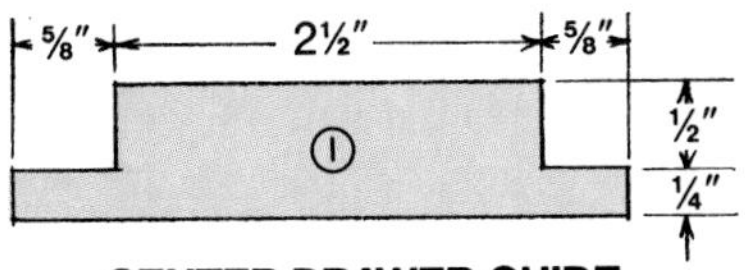

⅝" — 2½" — ⅝"

I

½"
¼"

CENTER DRAWER GUIDE

With the tablesaw blade set at 10°, cut the bottom and top of the drawer front.

Cut the drawer-front ends with the blade set at 10°, and push the fronts through with a pushblock.

M and N as shown on the Drawer Layout Drawing, *opposite.*

3. Using a tablesaw with the blade set at 10° from vertical, cut the drawer fronts as shown on the Drawer Front Drawing, *above,* and in the photos, *above right.* (We test-cut scrap material first to check the bevel angle and the depth of the cut. Use a pushblock to push the fronts through when cutting the ends. You'll want to square up the edges after making the cuts.)

4. Again, using the tablesaw, cut a ½" rabbet ⅜" deep along the top and bottom of the back side of the drawer fronts (O) as shown on the Drawer Front Drawing. Use the same two-cut procedure to cut a 1" rabbet ⅜" deep along each end of each drawer front. Also, cut a ½" rabbet ¼" deep along one end of each of the drawer sides (M), and a ¼" groove ¼" deep in the drawer fronts (O) as shown on the Drawer Layout and Drawer Front drawings.

5. Glue and clamp each drawer together. (Don't glue the bottoms into the grooves; you want them

to float free.) Check for square. "Rack" into square, if necessary. Remove glue squeeze-out as before. After the glue dries, sand the drawers smooth.

6. To fit the drawers to the opening, set the drawer guides (H, I) on the drawer-guide supports (G). Set the drawers on the guides and mark the location of the guides. (The guides should hold the drawers so they slide easily and are square with the front frame.) Remove the drawers, drill pilot holes through the guides into the guide supports, then glue and screw the guides to the guide supports.

Build the tabletop

1. Rip and crosscut the pieces for the tabletop (Q). (We cut our boards 1" longer and ¼" wider than the finished dimensions. This allows a little extra for jointing the boards' edges and for squaring up the ends later. If you don't have a jointer or don't joint your boards, you'll want to cut the tabletop pieces [Q] to finished width initially.) Lay the boards side by side in the arrangement in which they will be glued, then draw a large triangle on the tabletop for ease in realignment during clamping.

2. Mark the location of the dowels along the joint lines (we staggered them as shown on the Cutaway View Drawing, page 35, and spaced them from 8" to 12" apart). Now drill ⅜" holes 13⁄16" deep in the tabletop pieces (Q). Glue, dowel, and clamp the tabletop together. Alternate the clamps on the top and bottom of the boards, and space the clamps about 6" apart across the length of the top.

3. After the glue has dried, remove the clamps and use a scraper to remove the excess. Sand both tabletop surfaces smooth. Trim the ends to the finished 48" length. With a beading bit and router, rout the front edge and both ends of the tabletop. Finish-sand the tabletop.

Finish and assemble the table

1. Finish the base, drawers, and top separately (be sure to apply finish to both the top and bottom of the tabletop).

2. With the tabletop and base upside down, position the tabletop (it overhangs the base front and sides by ¾" and the back by ¼"). Then fasten the tabletop to the base with #8 × 1¼" roundhead screws (see the Cutaway View Drawing).

3. Attach the furniture glides, then set the table upright. Attach the drawer pulls and install the drawers in the base.

WATERFALL END TABLE

Sleek, smooth, and very contemporary, this oak veneer end table speaks clearly, yet with warmth, about your good taste and your skill as a woodworker. A larger version of this same design will work equally well as a sofa table or buffet table.

Build the framework

1. Lay out and mark the framework parts (A, B, C) on the back side (opposite the face or good side) of the ¾″ plywood sheet as shown on the Cutting Diagram and as dimensioned on the Exploded View Drawing and in the Bill of Materials, all *opposite.* Cut the side panels (A) slightly oversized; then, to avoid chipping, clamp them face-to-face and make the finish cuts. With the pieces still clamped together, sand the edges flush to the layout line to get two identical pieces.

2. With the side panels lying facedown, rout a ¼″ rabbet ⅜″ deep on the inside and outside edges to house the plywood skin you'll apply later.

3. Cut the spreaders (B, C), cleats (D), and center support (E) to size. (The top spreader [B] sits flush with the bottom of the rabbet, and the cleats hold it there. See the Section View Drawing, *opposite.*) Measure to find the center of the cleats and the side panels, then glue, nail, and clamp the cleats to the panels. (We drove finish nails from the inside to prevent the cleats from slipping out of position during clamping.) After the glue dries, remove the clamps; glue, nail, and clamp the spreaders (B, C) in place.

4. Glue, nail, and clamp the support (E) to the bottom side of the cleats in the center of the table as shown on the Exploded View Drawing. (The support serves as a joining location and a nailing surface for the first layer of ⅛″ plywood on the underside of the table.)

Bill of Materials

Part	Finished Size			Mat.	Qty.
	T	W	L		
A side panel	¾"	16"	36"	OP	2
B spreader	¾"	10½"	24"	OP	1
C spreader	¾"	2½"	10½"	OP	2
D cleat	¾"	¾"	24"	P	2
E center support	¾"	1"	10½"	P	1
F* top panel	⅛"	11¼"	32½"	MVP	4
G* bottom panel	⅛"	11¼"	28½"	MVP	4

*Plywood panels are cut to the dimensions given above to ensure an overlap.

Material Key: OP—oak plywood, P—pine, MVP—mahogany veneer plywood.

Supplies: flexible oak veneer—exact size of top is 12"×62⅞" and of bottom is 12"×53¼" (remember to cut the pieces oversize for an overlap), brads, contact cement, wood putty, water-base stain, polyurethane.

EXPLODED VIEW

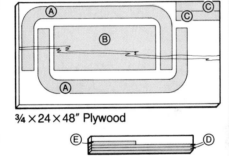

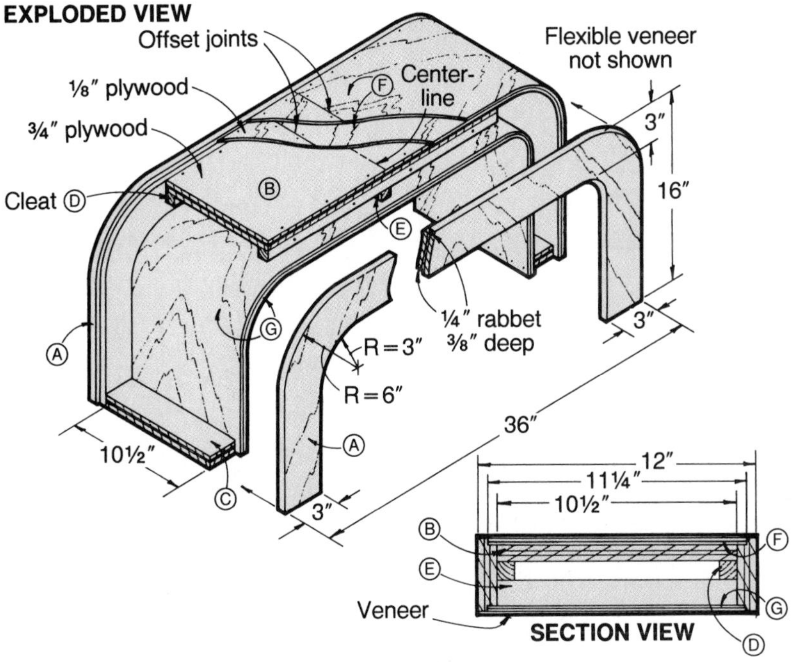

Offset joints
Flexible veneer not shown
Center-line
⅛" plywood
¾" plywood
Cleat Ⓓ
Ⓕ
3"
16"
Ⓑ
Ⓔ
¼" rabbet ⅜" deep
3"
Ⓐ
Ⓖ
R = 3"
R = 6"
36"
10½"
Ⓐ
Ⓒ
3"
12"
11¼"
10½"
Ⓑ
Ⓕ
Ⓔ
Ⓖ
Veneer
Ⓓ
SECTION VIEW

5. Cut the ⅛" mahogany veneer plywood panels (F, G) to width, then cut each panel to the length given in the Bill of Materials. This length allows for overlap on the ends, which you can trim off later. (We used two layers of ⅛" plywood for the base to which the veneer is applied because of the flexibility needed to wrap the material around the curved ends of the frame.)

6. Find and mark the center of the table. Then tack two of the top panels (F) at that point with brads, lay a bead of glue along the length of the rabbets, and working out from there, glue and nail the top panels into the rabbet. Run a zigzag bead of glue over the first layer for adhesion to the second. Then apply the second layer of plywood over the first, offsetting the joint.

7. Using the same procedure as described in step 6, glue and nail the bottom panels (G) in place. (We had some trouble bending the panels around the curved ends on the bottom side of the table. We solved this problem by applying hot water to both sides of the panels at the point of

Cutting Diagram

Ⓐ Ⓒ Ⓒ
Ⓑ
Ⓐ
¾ × 24 × 48" Plywood

Ⓔ Ⓓ
¾ × 3½ × 24" Pine

curvature as shown in the photo *below*.) Clamp curved blocks, as shown in the photo, *continued*

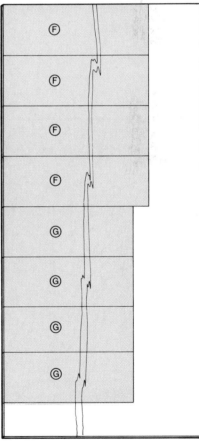

Ⓕ
Ⓕ
Ⓕ
Ⓕ
Ⓖ
Ⓖ
Ⓖ
Ⓖ
⅛ × 48 × 96" Plywood

WATERFALL END TABLE
continued

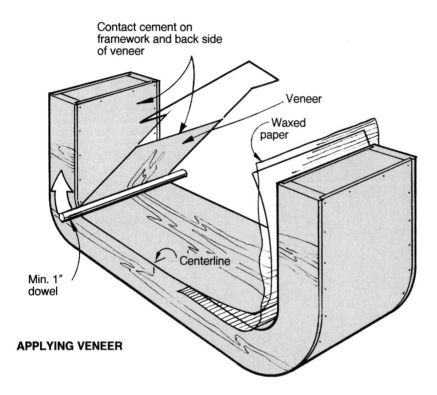

Contact cement on framework and back side of veneer

Veneer

Waxed paper

Centerline

Min. 1″ dowel

APPLYING VENEER

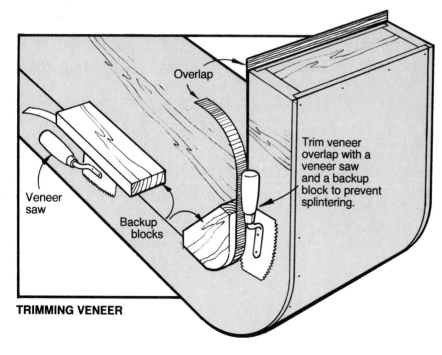

Overlap

Trim veneer overlap with a veneer saw and a backup block to prevent splintering.

Veneer saw

Backup blocks

TRIMMING VENEER

to pull the plywood into position on the inside curves. Then continue to glue and nail the rest of the plywood to the frame.

8. Trim the overlap of the plywood panels at the foot of each end. Fill all joints and nail holes with putty. Sand all surfaces smooth and flush, being careful not to round over the edges.

Apply the flexible veneer

1. Cut the oak veneer to size plus 1″ extra in all directions for an overlap on the ends and sides (finished size is stated in the supplies portion of the Bill of Materials, page 39). Mark the center of each piece of veneer for later positioning onto the frame.

2. Apply two coats of contact cement to the underside of the table and to the back side of the oak veneer.

3. Place waxed paper between the veneer and the frame (once the two mating surfaces come in contact with each other, there is no easy way to realign them). Starting at the center and working out from there, press the veneer into position, using a dowel as shown on the Applying Veneer Drawing, *upper left.* (We discovered that this is a two-person task. Things seemed to work better when one person held the veneer safely away from the plywood while the other rolled the veneer into position with the dowel.)

4. Trim the excess veneer, using a veneer saw and backup block as shown on the Trimming Veneer Drawing, *lower left.* Then lightly sand the veneer flush.

5. Apply and trim the top veneer using the same method you used on the bottom side.

6. Finish-sand, being extremely careful not to sand through the veneer or round off the edges. Stain, if desired, and finish with several coats of polyurethane. (We suggest a water-base stain.)

BURL-TOPPED
COFFEE TABLE

F or a long time now we've been fascinated by the intricate beauty of Carpathian elm burl. It's exquisite, especially after the finish has been applied. So, when we set out to select just the right wood for this coffee table's three veneered panels, it didn't take long to settle on this show-stopping species.

Add finely tapered legs with walnut-striped highlighting and solid mortise and notched-tenon construction and you have all the elements for an extraordinary project.

continued

BURL-TOPPED COFFEE TABLE

continued

Start with the legs

Note: *You'll need thick stock for the table legs. You can either laminate thinner stock to size or purchase turning squares. See the Buying Guide on page 45 for our turning-square source.*

1. Cut four legs (A) to size from 2″-square stock. Using the drawing *below* as a guide, lay out the location of the four saw kerfs on one end of each leg. To ensure the kerfs are cut to the right length, mark kerf-length reference lines opposite the faces in which the kerfs will be cut.

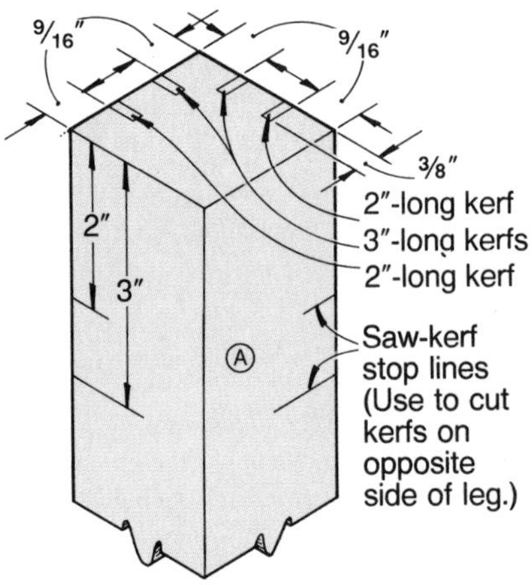

2. Adjust the rip fence on the tablesaw to cut the first kerf where marked, and raise the saw blade ¼″ above the surface of the saw table. With the saw turned off, slide a block of wood along the rip fence until it makes contact with the blade. Now, as shown in the drawing at *right,* make a mark on the inside face of the fence above this point of contact.

3. Clamp a stop to the rip fence 3″ behind the marked line. Cut the first 3″-long kerf in each of the four legs as shown in photo A, *above* (the inside cuts are 3″ long and the outside cuts are 2″ long). (You can use this setting

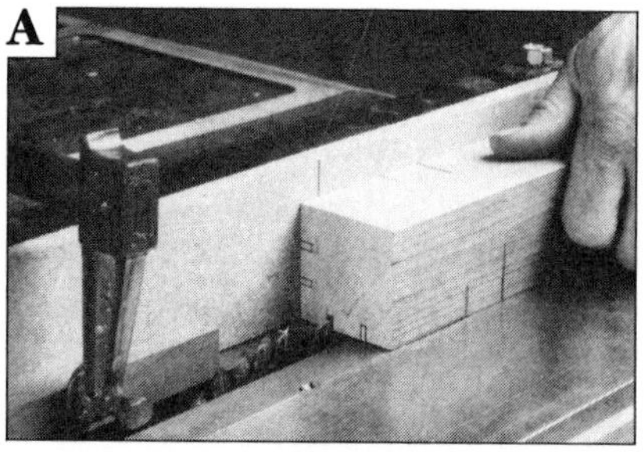

Cutting a kerf in the top end of the table leg on the tablesaw.

for cutting *one* of the kerfs in *each* leg. You'll need to move the fence *three* more times to cut the remaining three kerfs in each leg. Use the stop at the first setting for cutting two 3″-long kerfs in each of the legs. Reposition the stop 2″ from the mark on the rip fence to cut the 2″-long kerfs.)

4. To make the decorative inserts, cut a 42″-long strip of walnut to ⅛″ thick by 5/16″ wide. From the strip, cut eight pieces 3″ long and eight pieces 2″ long. Sand one end of each walnut insert to match the contoured end of the saw kerfs in the legs where shown on the Kerf Detail accompanying the Exploded View Drawing, *opposite.* Glue the inserts in place and sand them flush after the glue dries.

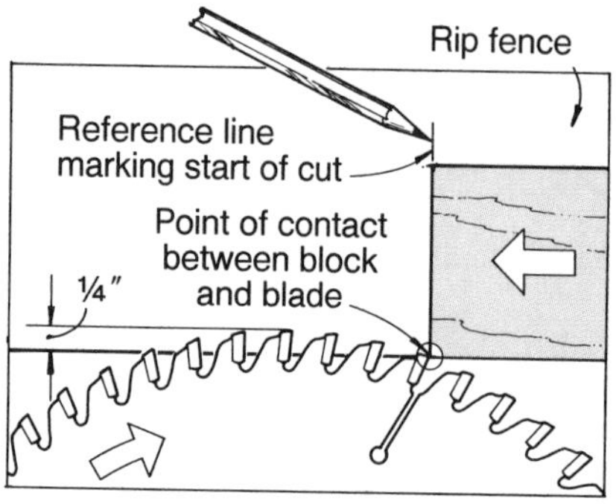

Bill of Materials					
Part	Finished Size*			Mat.	Qty.
	T	W	L		
A leg	2″	2″	16″	RO	4
B end rail	¾″	3½″	21⅛″	RO	2
C side rail	¾″	3½″	59⅛″	RO	2
D* end rail	¾″	2⅜″	21⅜″	RO	2
E* stile	¾″	2⅜″	60⅛″	RO	2
F* center rail	¾″	2¾″	17⅜″	RO	2
G* panel	¾″	17⅜″	17⅜″	PLY	3
H* veneer	1/64″	17⅜″	17⅜″	V	3

*Parts marked with an * are cut larger initially, then trimmed to finished size. Please read the instructions before cutting.

Material Key: RO—red oak, PLY—AB plywood, V—veneer.

Supplies: ⅛″ walnut for decorative kerfs and splines, #6×⅝″ flathead wood screws, #8×1¾″ flathead wood screws, #8×1¼″ flathead wood screws, polyurethane sanding sealer, polyurethane, 4—furniture glides, veneer glue.

5. To cut rabbets on the top end of each leg, use a dado set to cut a ⅜″ rabbet ¾″ deep on the *two kerfed* surfaces where shown on the drawing *below.*

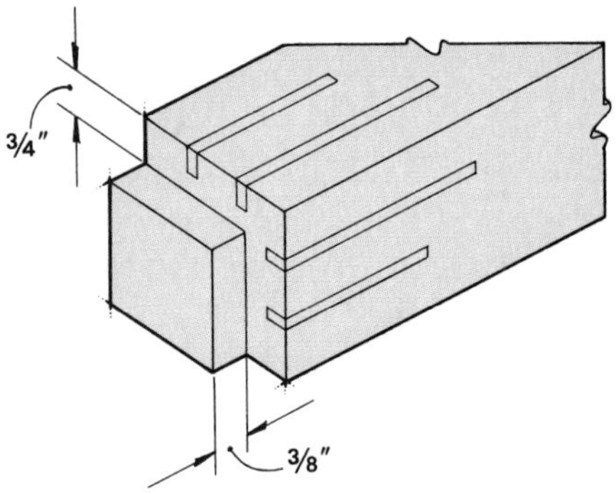

6. Referring to the Mortises Drawing, page 44, mark the location of a pair of mortises on each leg. Drill 5/16″ overlapping holes in the leg to rough-out the mortises. Then chisel the mortises clean. *continued*

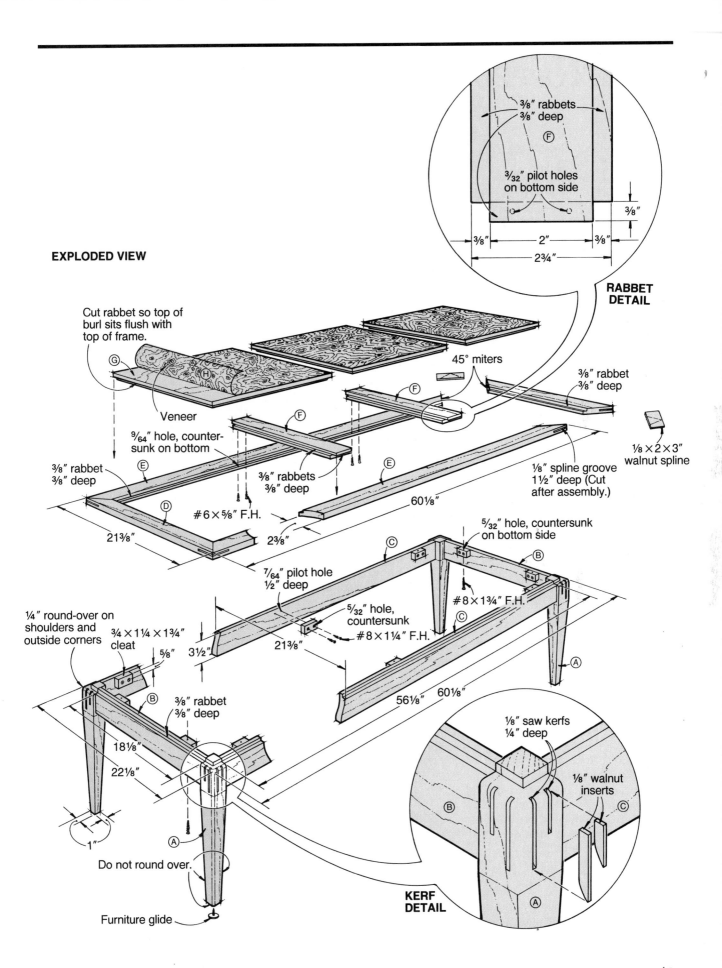

RABBET DETAIL

⅜" rabbets
⅜" deep

Ⓕ

³⁄₃₂" pilot holes
on bottom side

⅜"

⅜" 2" ⅜"

2¾"

EXPLODED VIEW

Cut rabbet so top of
burl sits flush with
top of frame.

Ⓖ

Ⓗ

Veneer

45° miters

Ⓕ

⅜" rabbet
⅜" deep

Ⓕ

⅛ × 2 × 3"
walnut spline

⁹⁄₆₄" hole, counter-
sunk on bottom

Ⓔ

⅜" rabbet
⅜" deep

Ⓔ

⅜" rabbets
⅜" deep

⅛" spline groove
1½" deep (Cut
after assembly.)

Ⓓ

#6 × ⅝" F.H.

60⅛"

21⅜"

2⅜"

⁷⁄₆₄" pilot hole
½" deep

⁵⁄₃₂" hole, countersunk
on bottom side

Ⓒ

Ⓑ

Ⓒ

#8 × 1¾" F.H.

¼" round-over on
shoulders and
outside corners

¾ × 1¼ × 1¾"
cleat

⅝"

3½"

⁵⁄₃₂" hole,
countersunk

#8 × 1¼" F.H.

21⅜"

Ⓐ

Ⓑ

⅜" rabbet
⅜" deep

56⅛"

60⅛"

18⅛"

22⅛"

1"

Ⓐ

Do not round over.

Furniture glide

⅛" saw kerfs
¼" deep

Ⓑ

⅛" walnut
inserts

Ⓒ

Ⓐ

KERF DETAIL

BURL-TOPPED COFFEE TABLE
continued

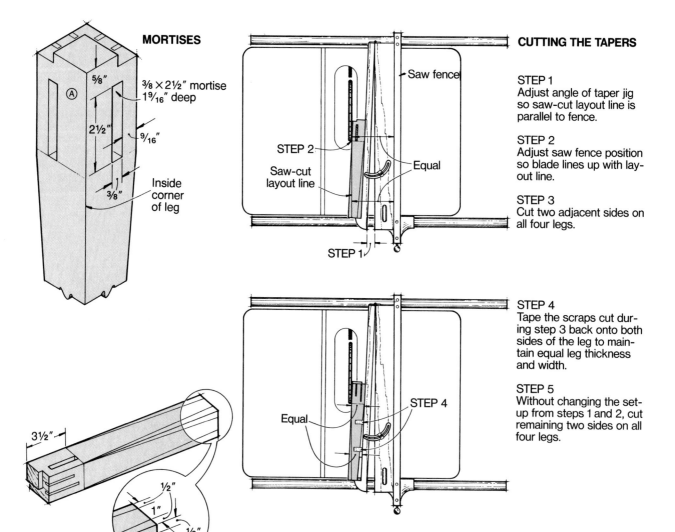

MORTISES

⅝"

Ⓐ

⅜ × 2½" mortise 1⁹⁄₁₆" deep

2½"

⁹⁄₁₆"

⅜"

Inside corner of leg

3½"

½"

1"

1"

½"

Saw fence

STEP 2

Saw-cut layout line

Equal

STEP 1

CUTTING THE TAPERS

STEP 1
Adjust angle of taper jig so saw-cut layout line is parallel to fence.

STEP 2
Adjust saw fence position so blade lines up with layout line.

STEP 3
Cut two adjacent sides on all four legs.

STEP 4
Tape the scraps cut during step 3 back onto both sides of the leg to maintain equal leg thickness and width.

STEP 5
Without changing the setup from steps 1 and 2, cut remaining two sides on all four legs.

Equal

STEP 4

8. Using a taper jig, cut the tapered legs to shape, following the sequence noted on the Cutting the Tapers Drawing, *top right*. Sand each tapered leg.

9. Mount a ¼" round-over bit to your table-mounted router. Rout along the outside corner and the two outside shoulders of each leg where shown on the Kerf Detail, page 43.

Add the rails

1. Cut the end rails (B) and side rails (C) to size. Lay out and cut a ⅜ × 1½"-long tenon on each

end of each rail (see the Tenons Drawing, *below*, for the needed dimensions). Cut the top 1" off each tenon. Now cut a ⅜" notch 1¼" long on the *top* end of each side rail and on the *bottom* end of each end rail.

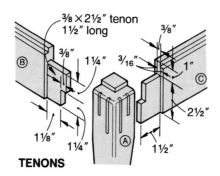

⅜ × 2½" tenon 1½" long

⅜"

Ⓑ

⅜"

1¼"

¾₁₆"

1"

Ⓒ

2½"

1⅛"

1¼"

Ⓐ

1½"

TENONS

2. Dry-clamp the rails to the legs, checking the fit of the tenons in the mortises. As shown on the drawing *below*, mark the size of the rabbet needed on the top outside edge of each rail. Cut or rout the rabbet to size along each rail.

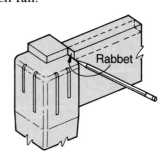

Rabbet

3. Glue and clamp an end rail between two legs to form each end subassembly and let dry. Later, glue and clamp the two side rails in position to form the table base, checking for square.

Make the tabletop frame
1. Cut the end rails (D), stiles (E), and center rails (F) to size *plus* 1″ in length.

2. Cut or rout a ⅜″ rabbet ⅜″ deep along the top inside edge of the end rails and the stiles and along both edges of each center rail where shown on the Exploded View Drawing, page 43.

3. Miter-cut the end rails and stiles to length. Using a band clamp, dry-clamp the frame together to check the fit. Then glue and clamp the frame.

4. Using a V-block jig like the one illustrated on page 24, cut a ⅛″ spline groove 1½″ deep centered on the frame as shown in photo B, *below*. (We used two people because it's too hard for one person to support the frame and make the cut.)

B

Cutting the spline groove with a V-block jig and a helper.

5. To form the splines, cut four pieces of ⅛″ walnut to 2×3″. Glue one piece in each corner groove. After the glue dries, trim off the excess, and sand smooth.

6. Cut the two center rails (F) to length to fit between the rabbets on the side stiles (E). Cut or rout a ⅜″ rabbet ⅜″ deep along the *bottom* of each center rail end.

7. Position the center rails between the stiles as dimensioned in the drawing *below*. Check for square. Using the hole sizes shown on the Exploded View Drawing, drill holes through the *bottom* of the side stiles and ¼″ into the *bottom* of the center rails. Glue and screw the rails in position. Sand the frame smooth.

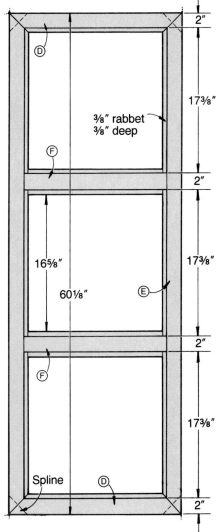

Make the panel inserts
1. Cut three pieces of ¾″ plywood (G) and three pieces of veneer (H) to 18×18″ (we used Carpathian elm burl veneer as listed in the Buying Guide).

2. Spread veneer glue on one face of the plywood and the back side of the veneer, following the instructions on the veneer-glue can. Position one veneer panel on each piece of plywood and press it down flat with a veneer roller.

3. *Carefully* measure *each* rabbeted-frame opening and cut the three plywood-veneer panels to size (we numbered the panels and frame openings to ensure that they matched up later). Cut or rout a ⅜″ rabbet on the *bottom* edge of each panel deep enough so the top surface of the veneer rests flush with or just *below* the surface of the frame.

4. Glue and clamp the panels.

Add the finishing touches
1. Finish-sand the base and top, being *extremely careful* not to sand through the thin veneer.

2. To attach the top to the base, start by ripping a strip of ¾″ stock to 1¼″ wide by 20″ long. Cut ten 1¾″-long cleats from the strip. Drill and countersink holes where shown on the Exploded View Drawing. Fasten the cleats to the base first, mounting them ¹⁄₁₆″ *below* the top edge of the rails. (This allows you to tighten the top snugly against the base.) Now center the top on the base, and screw it down.

3. Finish as desired. (We applied two coats of polyurethane sanding sealer, and then several coats of clear polyurethane, sanding lightly between coats.)

Buying Guide
• **Carpathian elm burl.** Paper-backed flexible veneer, cuts straight and clean with a crafts knife, lies smooth and flat with veneer glue. 18×96″ roll. Catalog no. FV22. For current price, contact Constantine's, 2050 Eastchester Rd., Bronx, NY 10461. Or call 800-223-8087.
• **Veneer glue.** One pint of contact adhesive, catalog no. 12VGP. Contact Constantine's (address above).
• **Red oak turning squares.** 2×2×18″. Contact Constantine's (address above).

PLASTIC-LAMINATE PARSONS TABLE

A single sheet of ¾" plywood and another of high-gloss laminate join forces in this easy-as-pie project. The finished product measures 36" square and 17" high—ideal for a conversation grouping like this one. Or, adapt our dimensions to suit your specific requirements.

Build the plywood frame

1. Lay out all the parts of the frame on the face side of the plywood, as shown on the Cutting Diagram, page 48. Then, with a tablesaw (and a helper if you can find one), cut the top (A) to size.

2. Using the Cutting Diagram as a reference, rough-cut the table legs (B, C) with a jigsaw. Then trim the exterior edges and the leg bottoms with the tablesaw.

3. To make the interior cuts on B and C perfectly straight, attach a long wooden auxiliary fence to your tablesaw fence. Unplug the tablesaw, raise the blade to its full height, and position the fence against the blade. Slide a piece of wood along the fence until it comes into contact with the blade, and mark the maximum length of the blade cut on the wooden fence, as shown on the Marking the Length of the Blade Cut Drawing, *upper right.* Extend these lines up the side of the wooden fence so that they will be visible when you cut the plywood.

4. Using a straightedge, mark start and stop lines on each A and B, as shown on the Cutting Diagram, page 48. Now move the tablesaw fence 2¼″ away from the inside edge of the blade. Lower the blade below the surface of the table, and set one of the B legs on the surface of the saw. Line up the start and stop lines on B with those on the wooden fence, and clamp start blocks and stopblocks to the fence at those points (see photo A, *right*).

5. With one of the Bs against the auxiliary fence and the start block, plug the tablesaw in and turn it on. Slowly raise the rotating blade up through the ¾″ plywood stock until the blade is extended upward to its full cutting height. The blade is not only at its full cutting height, but also at its full cutting length as measured in step 3.

Warning: *When raising the moving blade through the plywood, be sure to hold the plywood firmly against the table; do not, though, put your hand near the area where the blade will protrude through the surface!*

MARKING THE LENGTH OF THE BLADE CUT

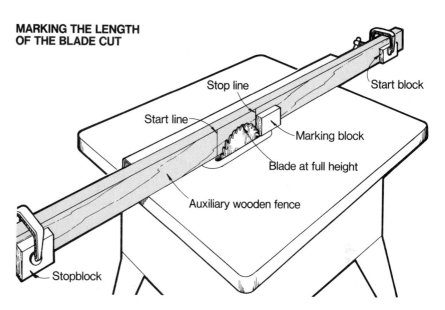

Stop line · Start block · Start line · Marking block · Blade at full height · Auxiliary wooden fence · Stopblock

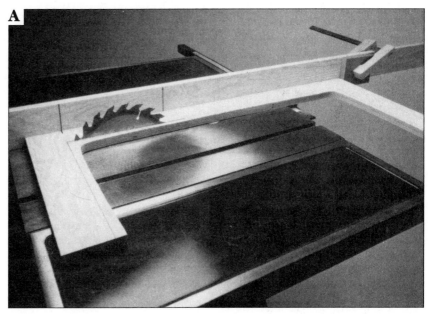

A

6. Push the leg along the fence until you meet the stopblock at the other end of the fence (see photo B, page 49). Holding B in place, shut off the saw and wait until it comes to a complete stop before removing the piece. Lower the blade, place the other B in position, raise the blade through it, and cut it in the same manner. To cut the C legs (they are ¾″ narrower), you will need to move each stopblock toward the center by ¾″.

7. To make the cuts along the legs of B, move the fence 3″ from the inside edge of the blade. Position a *continued*

PLASTIC-LAMINATE PARSONS TABLE
continued

LAMINATING SEQUENCE

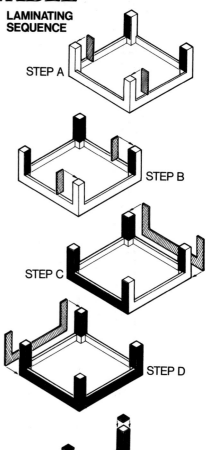

STEP A

STEP B

STEP C

STEP D

STEP E

EXPLODED VIEW

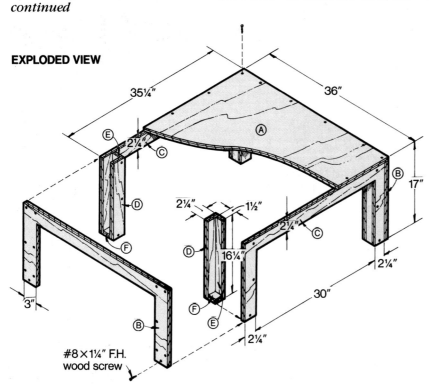

35¼"

36"

2¼"

17"

2¼"

1½"

2¼"

16¼"

2¼"

30"

3"

2¼"

#8 × 1¼" F.H. wood screw

Cutting Diagram

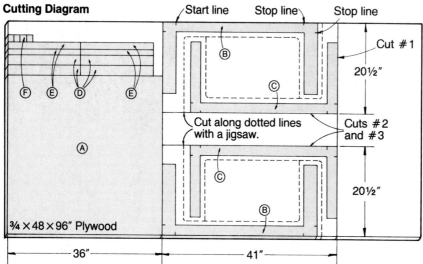

Start line

Stop line

Stop line

Cut #1

20½"

Cut along dotted lines with a jigsaw.

Cuts #2 and #3

20½"

¾ × 48 × 96" Plywood

36"

41"

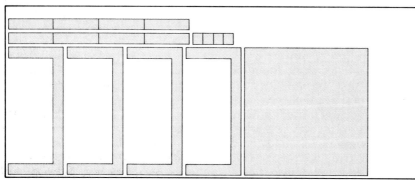

48 × 120" Laminate

Bill of Materials

Part	Finished Size*			Mat.	Qty.
	T	W	L		
A top	¾"	36"	36"	PLY	1
B* leg	¾"	16¼"	36"	PLY	2
C* leg	¾"	16¼"	34½"	PLY	2
D inner leg	¾"	2¼"	16¼"	PLY	4
E inner leg	¾"	1½"	16¼"	PLY	4
F inner leg	¾"	1½"	1½"	PLY	4

*Parts marked with an * are cut larger initially, then trimmed to finished size. Please read the instructions before cutting.

Material Key: PLY—plywood.
Supplies: #8 × 1¼" flathead wood screws, wood filler, contact cement, 1—4 × 8' sheet of plastic laminate, black paint, petroleum jelly, permanent black felt-tipped marker.

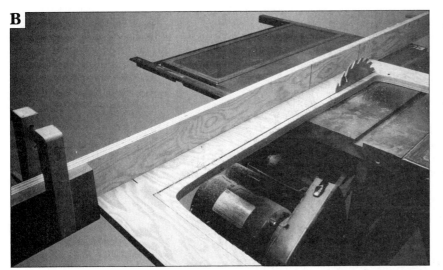

B

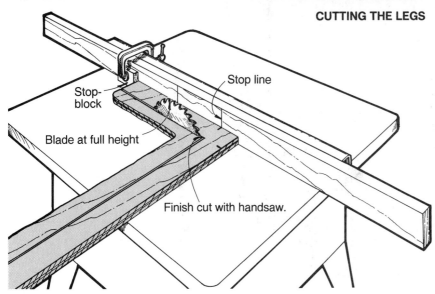

CUTTING THE LEGS

Stop-block

Stop line

Blade at full height

Finish cut with handsaw.

stopblock on the fence, and cut both inside cuts on each B as shown on the Cutting the Legs Drawing, *above.* Move the fence 2¼″ from the blade, and make both cuts on the inside edge of each C using the same stopblock. You will need to use a handsaw to square up the cuts, as the blade leaves an arc-shaped cut.

8. Dry-clamp the leg assemblies (B–C) together, and check for a proper fit of all the parts. Trim if necessary. Then glue and clamp the leg assemblies together, checking for square. Be careful not to round over or dent the square edges when clamping. To reinforce the joints, drill pilot holes and drive #8 × 1¼″ flathead wood screws where shown on

the Exploded View Drawing, *opposite, top left.* Make sure the head of each screw rests flush with the surface of the plywood (otherwise, the screws will show through when you apply the plastic laminate).

9. Glue and clamp the tabletop onto the leg assembly and secure it with screws.

10. For the inner legs, cut the plywood parts D, E, and F to the sizes given in the Bill of Materials. Glue up one D, one E, and one F for each inner leg. Secure the pieces together with #8 × 1¼″ flathead wood screws.

11. Glue and screw the inner-leg assemblies to the table assembly to form the completed plywood carcass.

12. After the glue dries, fill *all* voids and holes with filler. Sand the carcass assembly smooth, being extremely careful not to round over any edges.

Apply the laminate
1. Using the Laminating Sequence Drawing, *opposite, top right,* as a guide, cut and apply laminate to the inner edges of each leg (see steps A and B).

To adhere the plastic laminate to the plywood, give both the bottom side of the first piece of laminate and the mating plywood surface a liberal coat of contact cement (use only the nonflammable type). Allow the adhesive to dry. (If the adhesive sticks to your finger when you touch it, it's not ready.) Be sure to position the laminate accurately on the plywood; it's nearly impossible to adjust it once the two surfaces make contact. Using a rubber J-roller and a lot of pressure, pass the roller over the entire surface to ensure a good bond between the laminate and the plywood.

2. Lower the table onto the face side of the laminate, and trace the outline of the legs and tabletop with a colored grease pencil. When cutting, allow at least ½″ overlap in all directions. This will be trimmed with a router later. Apply the laminate to the plywood legs as shown on steps C and D, then to the tabletop, and then to the bottom of the legs (Step E). Trim after each step with a router fitted with a flush-cutting bit. (We rubbed petroleum jelly along the path of the bit's pilot to prevent it from marring the already-applied laminate. The pilot may clog with glue and burn the laminate.)

3. To minimize the seam lines of the laminate, "stain" the exposed laminate edges with a permanent black felt-tipped marker. Wipe off the excess with a clean rag.

4. Mask off the laminate and paint black the remaining exposed plywood on the bottom side of the table.

KID-SIZE PICNIC TABLE

If you get a kick out of seeing kids' faces light up with delight, wait until you give that special someone this special something. Just the right size for a cookout with Mom and Dad, or for a little summertime tea-partying or bubble-blowing, this durable creation requires only four 16-foot 2×4s and a few dollars' worth of hardware.

Note: We used pressure-treated lumber for this project, but you can use redwood, cedar, or cypress with equal success. The wood you choose depends on the final look you prefer and your budget for this project. Cut the pieces as indicated on the Cutting Diagram, opposite, top, to get all the parts from four 2×4s.

Assemble the tabletop

1. Using 2×4 stock, cut the tabletop pieces (A) and tabletop supports (B, C) to length. Trim the bottom ends of the tabletop supports at a 45° angle as shown on the Exploded View Drawing, *opposite, center.* Cut the angled aluminum stock to size and file off any sharp edges.

2. Rip a strip of scrap stock to ⅝", then cut it into 2" lengths for later use as spacers.

3. Set the ¾" pieces of aluminum that you cut in step 1 on each side of each tabletop support (B). Drill pilot holes and screw the aluminum to the supports using #8×1¼" wood screws.

4. Choose the best face of the top pieces (A) and lay them facedown on the floor. Insert the scrap spacers between the tabletop pieces, and clamp the assembly together (make sure the ends of A are flush). Position the tabletop supports (B) 7" in from each end of the tabletop, then, using #8×1¼" wood screws, fasten the two supports to the tabletop.

5. Mark the center between the supports, then position and screw the center support (C) to the underside of the table at that point with #10×2" wood screws.

Attach the legs

1. Cut the seat supports (D) and seats (E) to length; cut the legs (F) to length plus 2". Then fashion the diagonal braces (G) by crosscutting a 2×4 piece to 20" and ripping it in half.

2. Cut one end of each leg (F) at a 38° angle, then cut the other end at the same angle to a finished overall length of 27¼".

3. Cut a ¾" rabbet ¼" deep on the top outside end of each of the legs to allow room for the angled aluminum that's mounted to the supports. (We clamped the legs to the radial-arm-saw table and used a dado blade to make the rabbet. You can also make the rabbet with a mallet and chisel, or with a router fitted with a straight bit.)

4. Position the two legs on a flat surface flush against a straight

2×4 or a wall, as shown on the Leg Marking Drawing, *below.* Now measure up 9″ on each leg and mark the location of the top of the seat support (D). Center the seat supports on the legs, then drill ¼″ holes and attach the supports to the legs.

Cutting Diagram

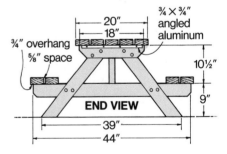

4—2×4″×16′ Treated Lumber

LEG MARKING

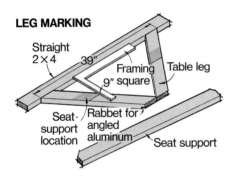

Complete the assembly

1. Clamp the leg assemblies to the inside of the tabletop supports and drill ¼″ holes through the tabletop supports and the legs. Fasten the legs to each of the supports with ¼×3½″ carriage bolts.

2. Clamp the seats (E) to the seat supports (see the End View Drawing, *far right,* for positioning). Drill ¼″ holes through the supports and seats, then fasten the seats to the supports using two ¼×5½″ carriage bolts for each seat board.

3. To further stabilize the table, cut each end of the braces (G) to 45° and to length to fit between the center brace and seat supports. Drill pilot holes and connect the pieces with #10×2″ wood screws.

4. Using a belt sander or sanding block, round over all sharp edges. Finish, if desired, or let the wood age naturally.

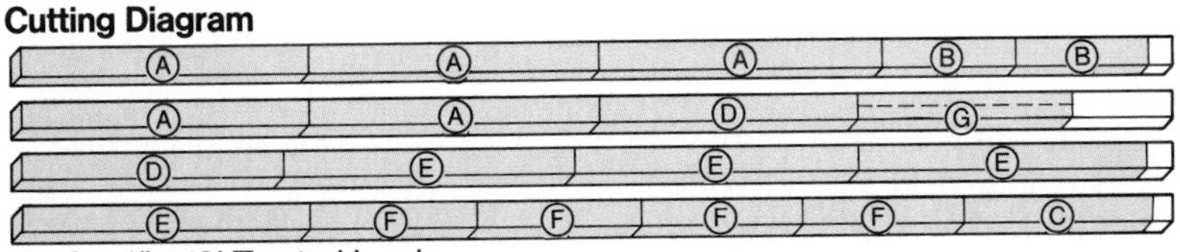

EXPLODED VIEW

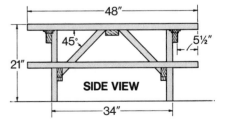

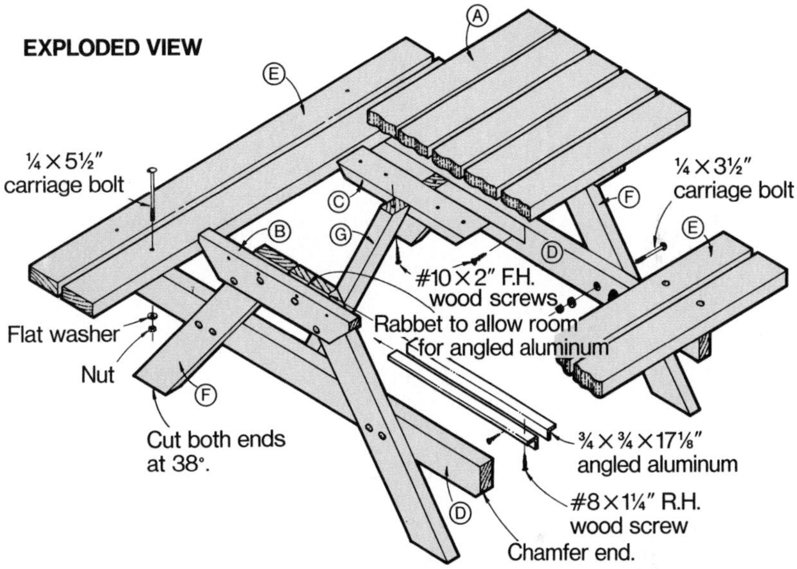

Bill of Materials				
Part	Finished Size*			Mat.	Qty.
	T	W	L		
A tabletop	1½″	3½″	48″	TL	5
B tabletop support	1½″	3½″	18″	TL	2
C tabletop support	1½″	3½″	18″	TL	1
D seat support	1½″	3½″	44″	TL	2
E seat	1½″	3½″	48″	TL	4
F* leg	1½″	3½″	27¼″	TL	4
G* brace	1½″	1½″	16½″	TL	2

*Parts marked with an * are cut larger initially, then trimmed to finished size. Please read the instructions before cutting.

Material Key: TL—treated lumber.
Supplies: 36—#8×1¼″ R.H. wood screws, 8—#10×2″ F.H. wood screws, 8—¼×5½″ carriage bolts, 16—¼×3½″ carriage bolts, 24—¼″ flat washers, 24—¼″ nuts, 4 pieces—⅛×¾×¾″ angled aluminum stock cut to 17″ (available at most hardware stores).

ACCESSORIES

The projects that follow start with the gem of a jewelry case shown above, then go on to show you how to try your hand and tools at no fewer than four terrific timepieces, a tulip-shaped torchère floor lamp, and a looking glass that has colonial class.

WALNUT JEWELRY CASE

Any woman appreciates having a special place to keep her small jewelry pieces neatly organized—especially when the unit looks as exquisite as its contents. Routed drawer pulls and handles of bird's-eye maple help put the walnut jewelry case shown *opposite* in a class by itself.

Make the frames

Note: You'll need some thin stock for this project. You can resaw your own or order it. See the Buying Guide on page 58 for our source.

1. Cut all the rails (A) and stiles (B) for the divider, side frames, and doors to the sizes listed in the Bill of Materials and on the Cutting Diagram, page 54.

2. Mark the half-lap joints on the rails and stiles where shown on the Frame Drawing, *below.* Then use a dado blade on your tablesaw or radial-arm saw to test-cut the joints. Adjust, if necessary, and cut the half laps.

FRAME (5 required)

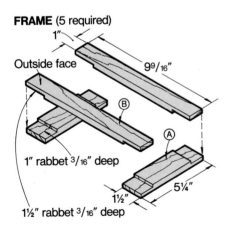

3. Glue and clamp the rails and stiles into five frames (two for the doors, two for the sides, and one for the divider), checking to be sure each is square.

TOP AND CAROUSEL
(As viewed from the bottom and back)

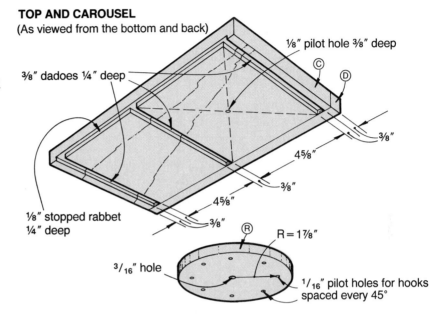

4. Rip the two side frames and the divider to 4⅞". Then rip the opposite stile of the divider for a 4¾" finished width. Finally, cut a notch for the magnet in the divider, and sand each of the frames smooth.

5. Rout ¼" rabbets ¼" deep in the openings in the back face of the two side frames, the divider, and the two doors. Square the corners with a chisel. Rout a ¼" rabbet ⅛" deep along the back edges of the side frames.

6. Take the frames to a glass dealer and have the mirror for the divider cut, as well as the glass for the left side and doors. (We had our pieces cut 1⁄16" less in both length and width to allow for contraction of the wood frames.) Also, have the glass dealer cut the 4½×9" mirror panel for the back of the necklace compartment.

Machine the case top and base

Note: The parts for the top and base are cut extra wide so you can rip the front strips (D, F) from them. This simplifies cutting the stopped dadoes and rabbets.

1. From ¾" walnut, cut two pieces to 6×11⅛" for the top (C, D) and the base (E, F).

2. Rip a ¾"-wide strip from the front edge of the top to form part D. Then rip a ⅜" strip from the front edge of the base to form part F. Finally, rip the top (C) and the base (E) to finished width (4⅞").

3. Cut ⅜" dadoes ¼" deep in the top and base where dimensioned on the Exploded View Drawing, page 55, and Top and Carousel Drawing, *above.* Next, cut the ⅜" rabbets ¼" deep on each end of the base. *continued*

WALNUT JEWELRY CASE
continued

Cutting Diagram

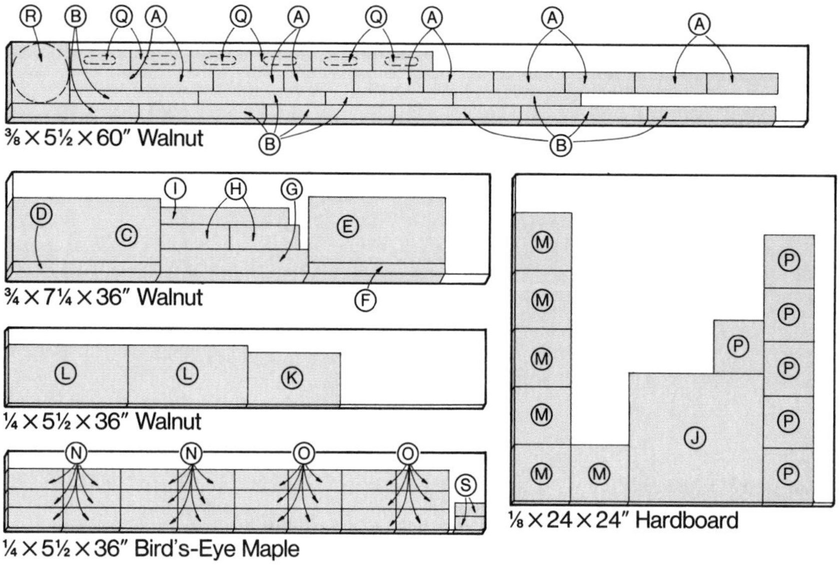

R B Q A Q A Q A A A
B B
⅜ × 5½ × 60" Walnut
D C I H G E F
¾ × 7¼ × 36" Walnut
L L K
¼ × 5½ × 36" Walnut
N N O O S
¼ × 5½ × 36" Bird's-Eye Maple
M M M M M M J P P P P P P
⅛ × 24 × 24" Hardboard

4. Rout a ⅛" rabbet ¼" deep along the back edge of the base (see the Exploded View Drawing, *opposite*). Rout a stopped rabbet the same size in the top where shown on the Top and Carousel Drawing, page 53. (We clamped stops to our router table fence to ensure that we stopped the rabbet at the right points when rabbeting the top.)

5. Glue part D to C, making certain that the ends of the two parts are flush. Then glue part F to E. Later, sand all surfaces flush.

Cut the top and base moldings

1. Start by cutting a strip of ¾" walnut to 1¾ × 24" for the base molding. (You'll cut parts G and H to length from this strip later.)

2. Rout the top (C, D) following steps 1, 2, and 3 on the Shaping the Top Molding Drawing, *below*. To form the molding for the bottom (G, H), follow steps 1 and 2 *only*.

3. Finally, cut a ¾" rabbet ⅜" deep along the base molding to house the base (E, F). Set the molding strip aside. *continued*

Bill of Materials

Part	Finished Size* T	W	L	Mat.	Qty.
A rail	⅜"	1½"	5¼"	W	10
B stile	⅜"	1"	9 9/16"	W	10
C* top	¾"	4⅞"	11⅛"	W	1
D top	¾"	¾"	11⅛"	W	1
E* base	¾"	4⅞"	10⅜"	W	1
F base	¾"	⅜"	10⅜"	W	1
G* bottom	¾"	1¾"	11⅛"	W	1
H* bottom	¾"	1¾"	5⅝"	W	2
I back stretcher	¾"	1"	9⅝"	W	1
J back	⅛"	9 9/16"	10⅛"	HB	1
K right panel	¼"	3 11/16"	7"	W	1
L drawer upright	¼"	4¼"	9"	W	2
M drawer support	⅛"	4¼"	4⅜"	HB	6
N drawer side	¼"	1 5/16"	4¼"	M	12
O drawer end	¼"	1 5/16"	3 13/16"	M	12
P drawer bottom	⅛"	3 13/16"	4"	HB	6
Q drawer front	⅜"	1 7/16"	4½"	W	6
R carousel	⅜"	4⅜" diam.		W	1
S door handle	¼"	⅞"	2¼"	M	2

*Parts marked with an * are cut larger initially, then trimmed to finished size. Please read the instructions before cutting.

Material Key: W—walnut, HB—hardboard, M—bird's-eye maple.
Supplies: #8 × ¾" roundhead brass wood screws, 3/16" flat washers, 8—½" brass cup hooks, double-faced tape, refrigerator magnet, 2—1" × #17 flathead nails, epoxy, clear silicone sealant, ⅛" glass, ⅛" mirror, finish.

SHAPING THE TOP MOLDING

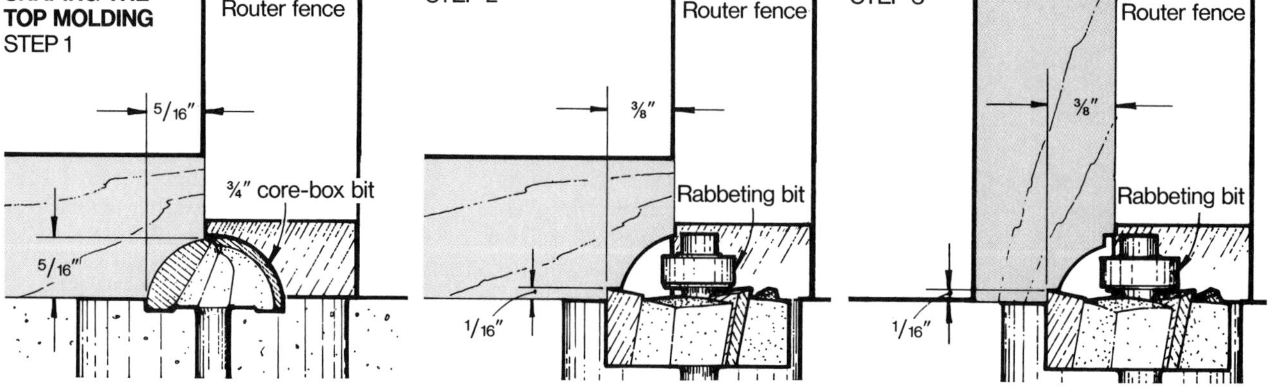

STEP 1
Router fence
5/16"
¾" core-box bit
5/16"
STEP 2
Router fence
⅜"
Rabbeting bit
1/16"
STEP 3
Router fence
⅜"
Rabbeting bit
1/16"

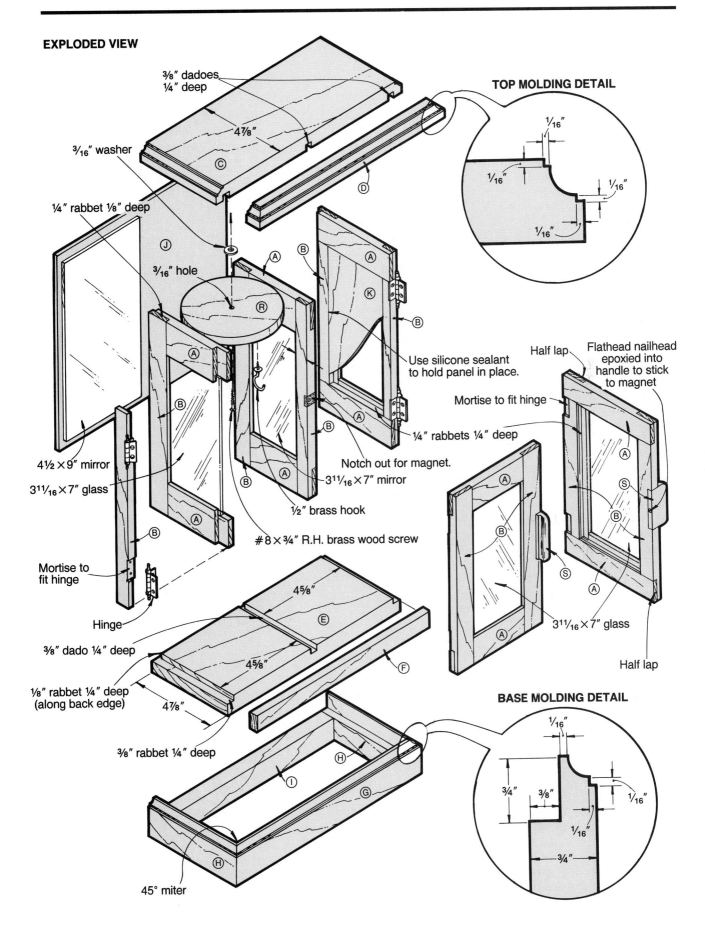

EXPLODED VIEW

⅜" dadoes
¼" deep

4⅞"

ⓒ

ⓓ

TOP MOLDING DETAIL

1/16"

1/16"

1/16"

1/16"

3/16" washer

¼" rabbet ⅛" deep

ⓙ

3/16" hole

ⓐ

ⓑ

ⓐ

ⓚ

ⓑ

ⓑ

ⓡ

Use silicone sealant
to hold panel in place.

4½ × 9" mirror

3¹¹⁄₁₆ × 7" glass

ⓑ

ⓐ

ⓐ

ⓑ

ⓐ

ⓑ

ⓐ

Notch out for magnet.

3¹¹⁄₁₆ × 7" mirror

½" brass hook

#8 × ¾" R.H. brass wood screw

¼" rabbets ¼" deep

Half lap

Flathead nailhead
epoxied into
handle to stick
to magnet

Mortise to fit hinge

ⓐ

ⓢ

ⓐ

ⓢ

ⓑ

Half lap

3¹¹⁄₁₆ × 7" glass

ⓐ

Mortise to
fit hinge

ⓑ

Hinge

⅜" dado ¼" deep

⅛" rabbet ¼" deep
(along back edge)

4⅞"

ⓔ

4⅝"

4⅝"

ⓕ

⅜" rabbet ¼" deep

ⓗ

ⓘ

ⓖ

45° miter

ⓗ

BASE MOLDING DETAIL

1/16"

¾"

⅜"

1/16"

1/16"

¾"

55

WALNUT JEWELRY CASE
continued

FRONT VIEW
(Shown without doors)

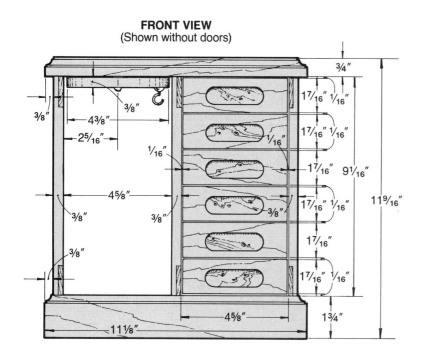

SIDE VIEW

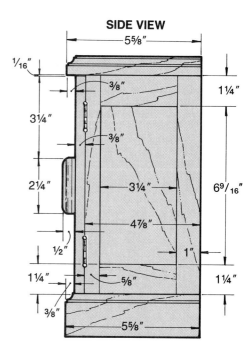

Complete the case

1. Referring to the Top and Carousel Drawing, page 53, locate the mounting hole for the carousel (R) by drawing diagonals on the bottom of the left-hand side of the top (C, D). Drill a ⅛″ pilot hole ⅜″ deep at the marked centerpoint.

2. Cut the hardboard back (J) to size. Glue and clamp the top, base, two side frames, and the divider together. Place the back in position, but do not glue it yet—it holds the case square.

3. Miter-cut the strip of base molding to length for parts G and H, and cut the back stretcher (I) to length. Then glue parts G, H, and I to the case.

4. Cut the right-side panel (K) to the size listed in the Bill of Materials and on the Cutting Diagram, page 54. Then apply a fine bead of clear silicone sealant to hold the panel to the frame (silicone sealant allows for expansion and contraction).

5. Using silicone sealant, attach the mirror to the divider.

DRAWER AND INSERT ASSEMBLY

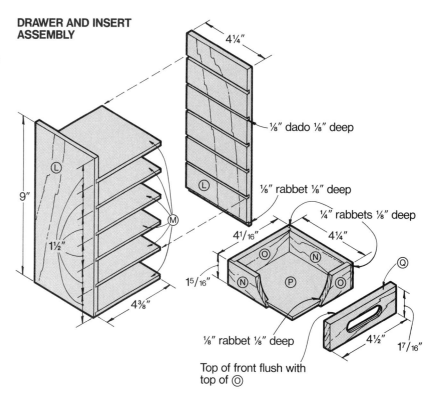

⅛″ dado ⅛″ deep

⅛″ rabbet ⅛″ deep

¼″ rabbets ⅛″ deep

⅛″ rabbet ⅛″ deep

Top of front flush with top of ⓞ

6. Cut the drawer uprights (L) to size. Then cut ⅛″-wide dadoes and a rabbet exactly where dimensioned on the Drawer and Insert Assembly Drawing, *opposite, bottom.*

7. Glue and clamp the uprights in the case (make sure they're flush with the back of the divider and side frame). Measure the length of the six drawer supports (M) so they fit snugly in the uprights. Cut the inserts to size, and glue them in place.

Build the drawers

1. Rip three 1⅝₆″ strips from ¼″ bird's-eye maple, as laid out on the Cutting Diagram, page 54, for the drawer sides (N) and ends (O). Cut a ⅛″ rabbet ⅛″ deep along one edge of each strip to accept the drawer bottoms. Finally, cut the drawer sides and ends to length (see the Bill of Materials).

2. Cut ¼″ rabbets ⅛″ deep along both ends of each of the drawer sides.

3. Cut six drawer bottoms (P) to size from ⅛″ hardboard.

4. Glue the drawers together, using a band clamp or rubber bands to hold each assembly together while the glue dries. Check each drawer for square while the glue is still wet.

5. After the glue has dried, remove the clamps and scrape off any excess glue. Sand each drawer smooth.

Make the drawer fronts

1. Make the walnut drawer fronts (Q) by cutting ⅜″ walnut to the dimensions listed in the Bill of Materials.

2. To form the finger pull in each front, start by making the template shown on the drawing at *right.* First, drill two 1″ holes 1¾″ apart on center through ¼″ hardboard. Then cut out the section between the holes with a jigsaw, and smooth the edge of the opening with a rasp and sandpaper. (Take your time when forming the opening on the template so you'll have pleasing results on the actual drawer

ROUTING THE DRAWER FRONTS

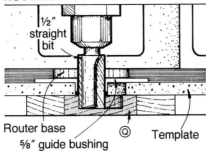

STEP 1. Make cut on back side of drawer front ⓠ first.

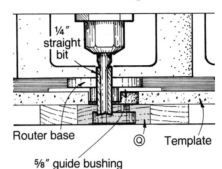

STEP 2. Make second cut on the front side of drawer front ⓠ.

fronts later.) Glue wood strips to the hardboard so that each drawer front will be held firmly in place and centered on the template opening.

3. Install a ⅝″ guide bushing to the base of your router. Then fit and adjust a ½″ straight bit in your router to make a cut ¼″ deep in the drawer front, as shown on step 1 of the Routing the Drawer Fronts Drawing, *left.* Rout out the recess on the back side of each drawer front.

4. Replace the ½″ bit with a ¼″ straight bit. Turn the drawer front (Q) over in the template and make the second cut, as shown on step 2 of the drawing.

Attach the drawer fronts and carousel

1. Slide the drawers into the drawer openings. The front surface of each drawer should be flush with, or slightly shy of, the front edge of the insert assembly (L, M). If not, *continued*

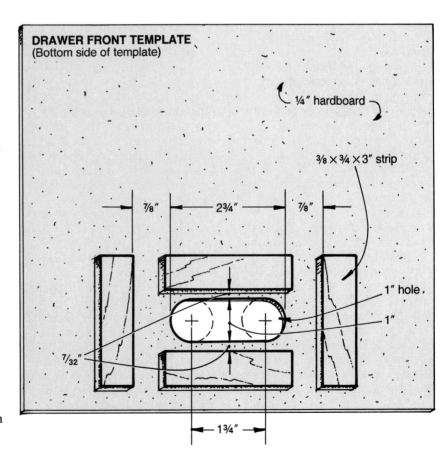

DRAWER FRONT TEMPLATE
(Bottom side of template)

¼″ hardboard

⅜ × ¾ × 3″ strip

⅞″   2¾″   ⅞″

1″ hole

1″

7/32″

1¾″

WALNUT JEWELRY CASE
continued

sand the drawer ends until you have a good fit.

2. Starting at the bottom and working up, glue and clamp a drawer front to the front of each drawer, centering each one from right to left and flush with the top edge (see the Front View Drawing, page 56, for proper clearance around each drawer front). If the spacing is too tight, just sand the edge of the drawer front down a bit. When you're finished, remove the case back (J) and spacers.

3. Make the carousel (R) by cutting a 4⅜"-diameter disk to shape from ⅜" walnut with a bandsaw. Sand the edges smooth. Then drill a ³⁄₁₆" hole through the center of the walnut disk and a ¹⁄₁₆" pilot hole for each brass hook, where shown on the Top and Carousel Drawing, page 53.

Fit the doors and make the handles

1. Using a tablesaw or small hand plane, size the doors by shaving equal amounts off opposite edges (be careful not to remove too much stock at one time). Fit the doors flush with the sides of the case. There should be a ¹⁄₁₆" gap between the two doors and between the doors and the top and bottom edges of the case.

2. Cut mortises for hinges in the doors and case where shown on the Side View Drawing, page 56. Now drill pilot holes for the hinge screws in both doors and sides (because the doors are so thin, use a stop on your drill bit). Check the length of the hinge screws against the thickness of the doors—you will probably need to shorten the screws with a file. Do *not* attach the doors yet.

3. To make the door handles (S), cut a strip of ¼"-thick maple to ⅞ × 8" (be sure to use a

FORMING THE HANDLES

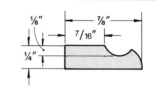

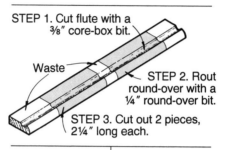

STEP 1. Cut flute with a ⅜" core-box bit.

Waste

STEP 2. Rout round-over with a ¼" round-over bit.

STEP 3. Cut out 2 pieces, 2¼" long each.

STEP 4. Fasten the 2 pieces together with double-faced tape.

Tape

STEP 5. Finish shaping by sanding a ½" radius on front corners.

pushblock when ripping to prevent kickback). Then follow steps 1 through 5 on the Forming the Handles Drawing, *above.* Use a dado blade in your tablesaw to cut a notch in each door for the handles (see the Side View Drawing for placement). Glue and clamp a handle to each door.

Apply the finish and assemble the jewelry case

1. Use masking tape and paper to protect the mirror in the divider. Then apply the finish of your choice to the drawers, doors, carousel, and case. (We sprayed on one coat of sanding sealer and followed up with two coats of lacquer. Whenever we use a spray-on finish, *especially* a lacquer, we always use a fume-respirator mask. The mask guards against vapors and dust.)

2. Fit the back (J) onto the case, mark the position of the mirror, and remove the back. Glue the mirror to the hardboard back. Glue the back to the case. (We used rubber bands to hold the back in position until the glue dried so as not to mar the finish.) Attach the glass panes to the left frame and the doors.

3. Screw the brass cup hooks in place, and attach the carousel to the case top with a screw and washer (the washer goes between the carousel and top). Leave the screw just loose enough so that the carousel turns easily.

4. Attach the doors and epoxy the magnet to the divider. Snip off all but ⅛" from two 1" × #17 flathead nails. Drill a pilot hole and epoxy the nailheads in place, one on each door, centered on the magnet. (When drilling the pilot holes, be careful *not* to drill through the door.)

5. Line the bottom of each drawer with velvet or felt. You also can custom-fit the drawers with dividers or padded compartments for storing rings and other accessories.

Buying Guide
• **Hinges.** Two pairs, ball-tipped, 1¼ × 1³⁄₁₆". Catalog no. H2200. For current price, contact Craftsman Wood Service, 1735 W. Cortland Ct., Addison, IL 60101. Or call 312/629-3100.
• **Thin stock.** ⅜" walnut, catalog no. W9725. ¼" bird's-eye maple, catalog no. W9112. Contact Craftsman Wood Service at the address or phone number above.

TWO EASY-TO-MAKE CLOCKS

Haven't built a clock before? It's never too late to start. Don't worry about the mechanical parts—you can order them from the sources listed in the Buying Guides, pages 60 and 61. Choose between a just-for-fun wall clock or a homey, old-time mantel clock. (And just in case neither of these timely projects strikes your fancy, we've included a couple more clock designs on pages 62–63 and 64–65.)

Angelfish Wall Clock

The things you can do with wood! By laminating curly maple with the edge grain up, we achieved a luminous look similar to that of a real fish.

Laminate the clock

1. Using ¾" curly maple, crosscut one 8"-wide piece 18" long. Then rip seven pieces ¾" wide from it. Now crosscut the 18" pieces in half. You now should have 14 pieces that each measure ¾ × ¾ × 9".

2. With the edge grain up, glue and clamp the pieces to form a rectangular lamination measuring 9 × 10½". Keep the surface of the lamination as flush as possible when clamping. After the glue dries, scrape off the excess, and belt-sand both sides smooth.

3. Using the dimensions listed on the Front View Drawing, *right,* lay out and mark the shape of the fish on the maple lamination. The lamination is extra large so you'll have excess on all edges.

4. To mark the position of the hour marks, use a compass to draw a circle with a 3¼" radius from the centerpoint. *continued*

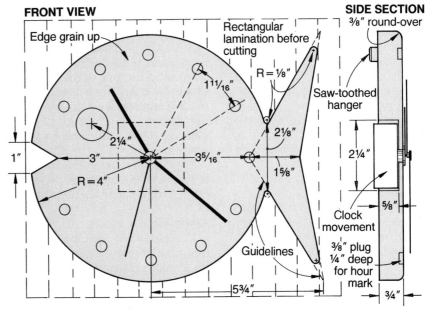

FRONT VIEW

Edge grain up

Rectangular lamination before cutting

R = ⅛"

$1^{11}/_{16}$"

2⅛"

2¼"

R = 4"

3"

$3^{5}/_{16}$"

1⅝"

Guidelines

5¾"

SIDE SECTION

⅜" round-over

Saw-toothed hanger

2¼"

Clock movement

⅜" plug ¼" deep for hour mark

5/8"

¾"

TWO EASY-TO-MAKE CLOCKS
continued

Bisect the centerpoint at 90° with two lines, one vertical and one horizontal, to mark 3, 6, 9, and 12 o'clock. Using a compass with the lead 1¹¹⁄₁₆″ from the compass point, mark points on the drawn circle to locate the position of the other hours. Now, referring to the Front View Drawing, page 59, mark the fish's eye.

5. Drill ⅜″ holes ¼″ deep for the hour marks. Then drill a ⁷⁄₁₆″ hole through the center of the 4″ radius to accommodate the shaft of the clock movement. Switching bits again, bore a 1″ hole ¼″ deep for the fish's eye.

6. Use a plug cutter to cut a 1″-diameter walnut plug ⁵⁄₁₆″ thick for the fish's eye. Using a ⅜″ plug cutter, cut 11 maple plugs ⁵⁄₁₆″ thick for the hour marks. If you don't have plug cutters, substitute dowel stock (remember, though, that dowel stock will show end grain and a plug will show surface grain).

7. Glue the walnut eye and maple hour marks in place. Sand the walnut and maple plugs flush.

8. Position the clock movement on the back of the lamination with the shaft inserted into the hole. Trace the outline of the clock onto the back of the lamination. Using a 1″ flat-bottomed bit (we used a Forstner), bore several holes ⅝″ deep to form the recess to house the clock.

Bore the recess slightly larger than the outline drawn. Clean out the corners and rough edges with a chisel and mallet. Check the fit of the clock in the recess and the shaft through the hole.

Form the shape
1. Using the guidelines shown on the Front View Drawing, page 59, mark and drill two ¼″ holes at the intersection of the body and tail. These holes create a smooth ⅛″ inside radius.

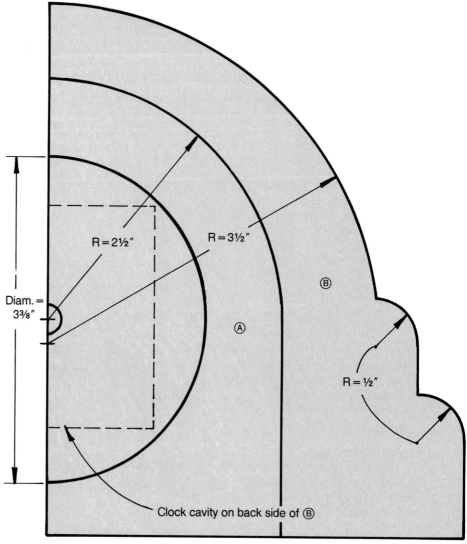

HALF-VIEW FULL-SIZED PATTERN

2. Using the lines previously drawn, cut the fish to shape. Then sand the tips of the tail to shape. (We taped sandpaper to a small-diameter dowel and mounted this in a hand drill to sand the small radii where the tail meets the body.)

3. Fit your router with a ⅜″ round-over bit, and rout the top edge, *except* the fish's mouth.

Assemble the clock
1. Finish-sand the clock. If you notice small gaps around the hour marks, inject a small amount of glue into the cracks and wipe off the excess with a wet finger.

Pack the glue-filled crack with fine maple sawdust with your finger (dry this time), and then continue to sand. The dust will make the crack nearly invisible.

2. Apply the finish. (We used two coats of gloss lacquer to highlight the curly grain.)

3. Attach a saw-toothed hanger, the clock movement, and hands.

Buying Guide
• **Quartz movement.** ⅝″ thick with a short shaft, catalog no. 10001. For current price, contact Klockit, P.O. Box 636, Lake Geneva, WI 53147. Or call 800-556-2548.

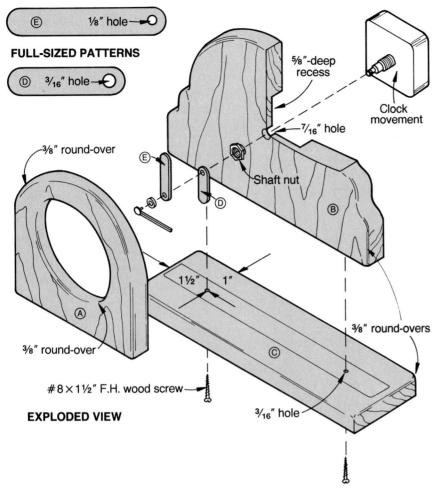

FULL-SIZED PATTERNS

(E) ⅛" hole

(D) 3/16" hole

⅜" round-over

(E)

Clock movement

5/8"-deep recess

7/16" hole

Shaft nut

(D)

(B)

1½" 1"

(C)

⅜" round-overs

#8 × 1½" F.H. wood screw

3/16" hole

(A)

⅜" round-over

EXPLODED VIEW

Bill of Materials					
Part	Finished Size			Mat.	Qty.
	T	W	L		
A front	¾"	5"	4¾"	O	1
B back	¾"	9"	5½"	W	1
C base	¾"	2¾"	9¾"	W	1
D hour hand	1/16"	⅜"	1¼"	O	1
E minute hand	1/16"	⅜"	1¾"	O	1

Material Key: O—oak, W—walnut.
Supplies: #8 × 1½" flathead wood screws.

Art Deco Mantel Clock

Just about everyone who's passed this clock in our offices has paused to admire it. Yet, it's almost embarrassingly fast and easy to make. We won't tell if you won't.

Build the clock body

1. Lay out and mark the oak front (A) and walnut back (B) as shown on the Half-View Full-Sized Pattern, *opposite*. Also cut the base (C) to the size indicated in the Bill of Materials.

2. Cut pieces A and B to shape with a bandsaw or jigsaw. Using a holesaw, bore a 3⅜" hole through A. (You also could drill a hole large enough for your jigsaw blade, and then cut a 3⅜" hole with the jigsaw.) Drill a 7/16" hole in B for the clock shaft.

3. Rout the front edges of A and B and the top edges of C with a ⅜" round-over bit. Drill and countersink two 3/16" pilot holes through the base where dimensioned on the Exploded View Drawing, *above*.

4. Position the clock movement on the back side of the walnut back (B) with the clock shaft in the 7/16" hole. Trace the outline of the clock on the back of B. Using a large-diameter flat-bottomed bit, drill 5/8"-deep holes to form a recess slightly larger than the drawn outline to house the clock movement. Check the fit of the clock in the recess, making sure that enough of the threaded shaft protrudes through B so you can fasten the shaft nut.

Make the hands

1. Resaw scrap oak stock to 1/16" thickness. (We cut enough thin stock for a few extra hands. It's a lucky thing we did because we broke one when drilling in a later step.) Stiff veneer stock also will work for the hands.

2. Using tracing paper and the full-sized patterns, *top left,* trace the hands (D and E) and hole positions onto the thin oak stock. Drill holes in both hands to fit the clock shaft.

3. Cut the hour hand (D) and minute hand (E) to length and sand to shape.

Assemble the clock

1. Finish-sand all clock parts, using extra care when sanding the hands.

2. Glue, clamp, and screw the back (B) to the base (C), then glue and clamp the front (A) to the base and back. Remove the excess glue.

3. Remove the clamps and do any necessary touch-up sanding. Finish the clock body and hands as desired (we sprayed on several coats of lacquer).

4. Install the clock movement and *carefully* attach the hands.

Buying Guide

• **Quartz movement.** 5/8" thick with a short shaft, catalog no. 10001. For current price, contact Klockit, P.O. Box 636, Lake Geneva, WI 53147. Or call 800-556-2548.

TURNED TEAK TIMEPIECE

Have you ever wondered what time it is in Hong Kong, Caracas, or Helsinki? In this day of high-speed jet travel and instant communications, it's often nice to know. The "world-time face" on our nautical-style wall clock makes it easy to tell the time for just about anywhere in the world at a glance. The quick-to-turn teak housing complements the polished brass for an eye-catching project that's sure to be noticed.

Form the clock lamination

1. Cut three pieces of ¾" teak to 8×8". Mark diagonals to locate the center of each. With a compass, draw a circle with a 2¹³⁄₁₆" radius on each square. Then draw another centered circle with a 3⅝" radius on *two* of the squares, and a 4"-radius circle on the *third*.

2. With a circle cutter chucked into a drill press, center and cut a 5⅝"-diameter (2¹³⁄₁₆"-radius) hole in each square. (Back with scrap stock to prevent chip-out, and clamp to the drill press.)

3. Cut the outside diameters of each square to a circular shape using a bandsaw. Now glue and clamp the three teak rings together with the inside edges flush. (Because teak is oily, we used resorcinol glue; epoxy also would work.)

Make the auxiliary faceplate assembly

1. From ¾" scrap, mark and cut two 6"-diameter disks. Drill a ⅜" hole through the center of each.

2. Center and screw one of the scrap disks to the lathe faceplate. Turn a rabbet on the front edge of the scrap disk—deep enough so that the teak lamination will fit snugly onto the rabbet.

3. Remove the rabbeted disk from the faceplate. Slip a ⅜×4½" carriage bolt through the back side of the disk. (If your faceplate doesn't have a center hole, you'll need to counterbore the back

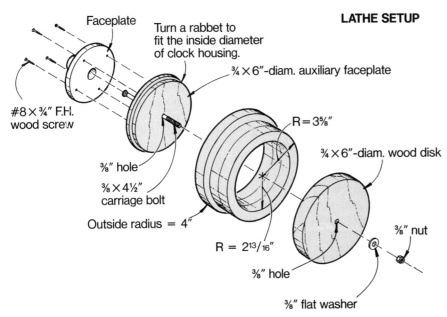

Faceplate

Turn a rabbet to fit the inside diameter of clock housing.

LATHE SETUP

¾×6"-diam. auxiliary faceplate

#8×¾" F.H. wood screw

R = 3⅝"

¾×6"-diam. wood disk

⅜" hole

⅜×4½" carriage bolt

Outside radius = 4"

R = 2¹³⁄₁₆"

⅜" hole

⅜" nut

⅜" flat washer

side of the rabbeted disk for the head of the carriage bolt.) Remount the disk to the faceplate.

Turn the clock body

1. Center and bolt the teak lamination between the disks as shown on the Lathe Setup Drawing, *opposite.*

2. Start the lathe, and true up the outside surface of the teak housing (we used a speed of about 1,000 rpm and cut it with a ½" gouge).

3. Make a template from the Full-Sized Pattern, *right.*

4. With the lathe running, lay the template up against the turning. Transfer the profile lines from the template to the teak lamination as shown in photo A, *below, near right.*

5. Using the lines as guides, turn the lamination to shape, stopping periodically to check the housing shape against that of the template. Turn to shape as shown in photo B, *far right.* Sand the lamination.

6. Remove the clock housing from the lathe. For hanging the clock later, drill a ³⁄₁₆" hole ½" deep at a slight upward angle where shown on the Final Assembly Drawing, *bottom right.*

7. Apply finish to the interior and exterior (we used polyurethane). To hold the clock movement to the teak housing, apply a small bead of silicone sealant to the back lip of the clock ring where shown on the Final Assembly Drawing. Install the battery and slip the clock movement into the cavity.

Buying Guide
• **World-time quartz clock movement.** Requires one "C" battery, catalog no. 15012. For current price, contact Klockit, P.O. Box 636, Lake Geneva, WI 53147. Or call 800-556-2548.

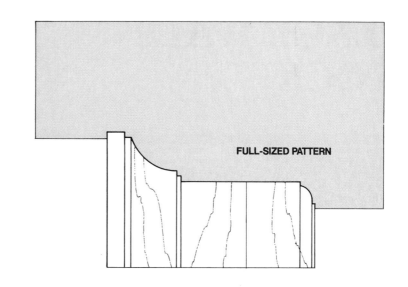

FULL-SIZED PATTERN

Mark profile lines on teak lamination with the lathe running.

Turn the lamination to shape using the marked profile lines as guides.

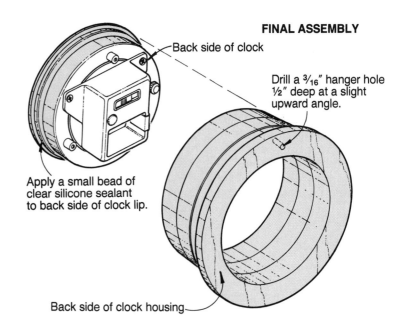

FINAL ASSEMBLY

Back side of clock

Drill a ³⁄₁₆" hanger hole ½" deep at a slight upward angle.

Apply a small bead of clear silicone sealant to back side of clock lip.

Back side of clock housing

WENGE WALL CLOCK

The bird's-eye maple face contrasts nicely with the African wenge frame and clock hands in this contemporary design from California craftsman Jim Payne. To make it easy for you to find the materials you'll need for this project, we've assembled a clock kit with the aid of the people at Constantine's. See the Buying Guide for details.

Construct the frame

1. Cut a piece of ¾"-thick stock to 1½" wide × 38" long. (See the Buying Guide for our source of wenge, or use walnut.)

2. Rout a ¼" round-over along one edge of the long strip.

3. Cut or rout a ⅜" rabbet ⅞" deep in the strip where shown on the Section View Detail accompanying the Exploded View Drawing, *opposite, top left.* Sand the long frame strip.

4. Miter-cut four frame pieces (A) to 8½" long each. Glue and band-clamp the frame pieces together, checking for square.

5. Apply masking tape on the frame front where shown in photo A, *opposite.* The tape is easy to mark on and minimizes chip-out when cutting the kerfs. Mark the ⅛"-wide kerf locations, and cut ⅛" kerfs ⅛" deep between the kerf lines. (We used a radial-arm saw, but you could place the frame facedown and cut the kerfs on a tablesaw.)

6. Rip a ⅛"-thick strip of maple from the edge of a ½"- or ¾"-thick board. With a handsaw or scrollsaw, cut a strip ³⁄₁₆" wide from the strip for the timing marks. (We'll narrow the ³⁄₁₆" width to ⅛" when we sand them flush with the frame.) Cut the hour marks to ¹³⁄₁₆" long, glue them in the kerfs, and sand them flush after the glue dries.

Veneer the face

1. Cut a piece of hardboard (B) to fit the rabbeted opening in the frame (we cut ours ¹⁄₁₆" undersize to allow for swelling and contracting of the frame).

2. Place the hardboard on the section of the veneer with the nicest figure (see the Buying Guide for our source of veneer). Use a utility knife to cut the veneer (see photo B, *opposite*). Peel off the backing sheet, then stick the veneer to the hardboard, keeping the edges flush.

3. Locate and drill a ⅜" hole in the center of the veneer face. (If you use a clock other than the one listed in the Buying Guide, measure the shaft diameter before drilling the hole.)

Form the hands

1. Rip a ⅛"-thick piece of wenge 12" long from the edge of a ¾"-thick board. Using carbon paper, transfer the Full-Sized Hand Patterns and hole centerpoints, *opposite, top right,* onto the thin strip.

2. Using a bandsaw or scroll-saw, cut the hands to shape. Drill a ³⁄₁₆" hole in the hour hand and a ⁵⁄₃₂" hole in the minute hand. Sand the hands to ¹⁄₁₆" thick.

3. With scissors or tin snips, cut the shaft end off the minute hand supplied with the clock (all you

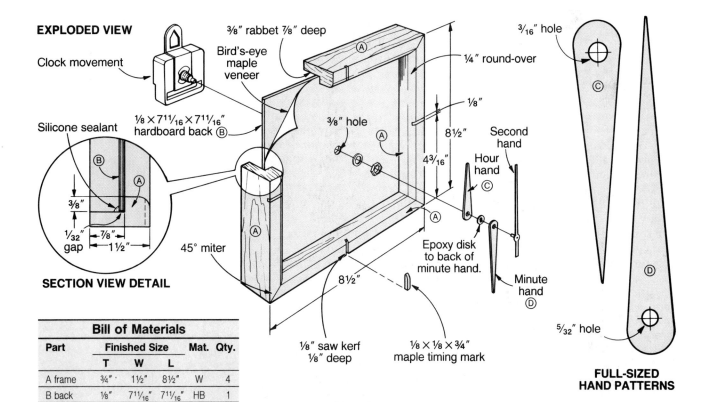

EXPLODED VIEW

Clock movement

⅜" rabbet ⅞" deep

Bird's-eye maple veneer

⅛ × 7¹¹⁄₁₆ × 7¹¹⁄₁₆" hardboard back Ⓑ

Silicone sealant

⅜" hole

Ⓑ

Ⓐ

Ⓐ

Ⓐ

Ⓐ

Ⓐ

⅜"

¹⁄₃₂" gap

⅞"

1½"

SECTION VIEW DETAIL

45° miter

¼" round-over

⅛"

8½"

4³⁄₁₆"

Second hand

Hour hand Ⓒ

Minute hand Ⓓ

Epoxy disk to back of minute hand.

8½"

⅛" saw kerf ⅛" deep

⅛ × ⅛ × ¾" maple timing mark

³⁄₁₆" hole

Ⓒ

Ⓓ

⁵⁄₃₂" hole

FULL-SIZED HAND PATTERNS

Bill of Materials				
Part	Finished Size		Mat.	Qty.
	T	W	L		
A frame	¾" ·	1½"	8½"	W	4
B back	⅛"	7¹¹⁄₁₆"	7¹¹⁄₁₆"	HB	1
C hour hand	¹⁄₁₆"	½"	2¾"	W	1
D minute hand	¹⁄₁₆"	½"	3½"	W	1

Material Key: W—wenge, HB—hardboard.
Supplies: epoxy, silicone sealant or glazier points, finish.

need is the end with the hole). As shown in photo C, *far right,* epoxy the disc, centered over the ⁵⁄₃₂" hole, to the back face of the minute hand.

Finish the clock, then add the movement

1. Apply the finish to the clock frame, hands, and veneered face. Later, use silicone sealant to hold the face in the frame (see the Section View Detail).

2. Fasten the clock movement to the veneered face, and slip the clock hands onto the movement's shaft. Add a battery and hang.

A

Mark the hour-mark locations and cut the kerfs.

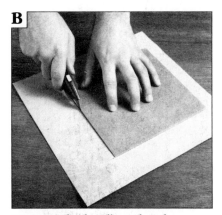

B

Position the hardboard and cut the veneer face with a knife.

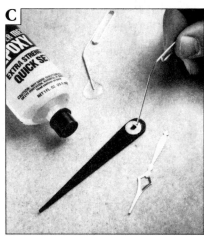

C

Epoxy the metal disc to the back of the minute hand.

Buying Guide
• **Wenge clock kit.** 12 × 12" bird's-eye maple peel-and-stick veneer, ¾ × 3 × 48" wenge, miniquartz clock movement. Catalog no. WD1188. To find out the current price, contact Constantine's, 2050 Eastchester Rd., Bronx, NY 10461. Or call 800-223-8087.

TORCHÈRE FLOOR LAMP

People in the home-furnishings industry call an accessory like this a torchère, a French word meaning torch holder. Regardless of what you call it, we think you'll find this floor lamp a stunning addition to your home's decor. It's everything a dark, uninspiring corner always wanted.

Note: You'll need some thin oak and walnut stock for this project. You can resaw or plane thicker stock to the correct thickness. See the Buying Guide, page 71, for our source of electrical parts for the lamp.

Build the base

1. Cut the base parts (A, B, C) to the sizes listed in the Bill of Materials. (If the dimensions in the Bill of Materials appear confusing, remember that we measure width across the grain and length with the grain.)

2. With the ends and edges flush, glue and clamp each of the eight base sections together, positioning the pieces where shown on the Base Section Drawing, *below.* Later, scrape off the excess glue. (Part C is used only to support each base piece when it is miter-cut to shape. Part C is cut from each base section during the miter-cutting process.)

3. Attach a wood auxiliary fence to your miter gauge where shown on step 1 of the two-step Miter-Cutting the Base Sections Drawing, *opposite.* To keep from cutting the fence in two when miter-cutting, make the fence at least 2″ high. Angle the miter gauge 22½° from center.

Note: Before cutting the eight base sections to shape as described in step 4 on the next page, we cut eight pieces of scrap hardboard the same size as part A (4⅝ × 5⅝″). Then we test-cut the eight hardboard pieces using the setup shown in steps 1 and 2 on the two-step drawing, opposite. Finally, we held the test-cut pieces together to check for gaps and verify the miter-gauge setting.

Bill of Materials

Part	Finished Size*			Mat.	Qty.
	T	W	L		
A base top	¾″	4⅝″	5⅝″	W	8
B base bottom	¾″	4⅝″	1″	W	8
C support	¾″	4⅝″	½″	W	8
D* column core	1½″	1½″	57″	LW	1
E* strip	¼″	⅝″	57″	W	8
F* shade section	¼″	3¼″	12″	O	8
G top ring	¾″	7¼″	7¼″	PLY	1
H bottom ring	¾″	1⅞″	1⅞″	PLY	1
I switch knob	¼″ diam.		1⅝″	WD	1

*Parts marked with an * are cut larger initially, then trimmed to finished size. Please read the instructions before cutting.

Material Key: W—walnut, LW—laminated walnut, O—oak, PLY—plywood, WD—walnut dowel.

Supplies: #8×2″ flathead wood screws, #8×1¼″ flathead wood screws, #8×¾″ flathead wood screws, epoxy, masking tape, aluminum foil, finish, three-way A lamp (30–70–100 watt).

BASE SECTION

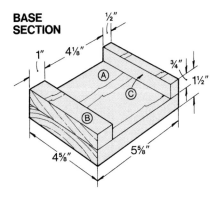

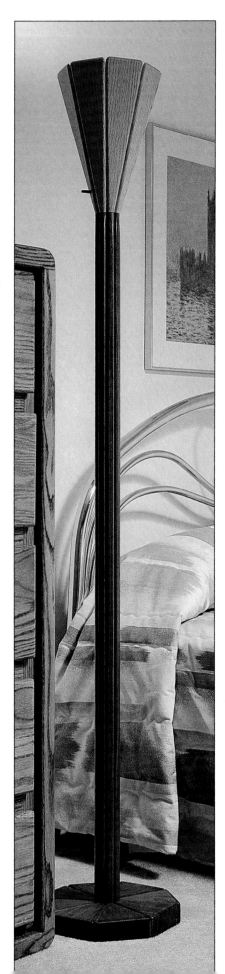

4. Mark a centerline on one end of one base section (see step 1 on the two-step drawing for location). Being careful to keep the clamp holding the stop out of the saw blade's path, align the blade with the marked line, set the stop, and cut the base sections to shape. Refer to the two-step drawing for details.

5. Using a ¼" round-over bit, rout each pie-shaped base section where shown on the Exploded View Drawing, *right*. (We routed ours on a table-mounted router fitted with a fence.) Sand each base section.

6. Glue and "clamp" four of the sections together on a piece of plywood covered *continued*

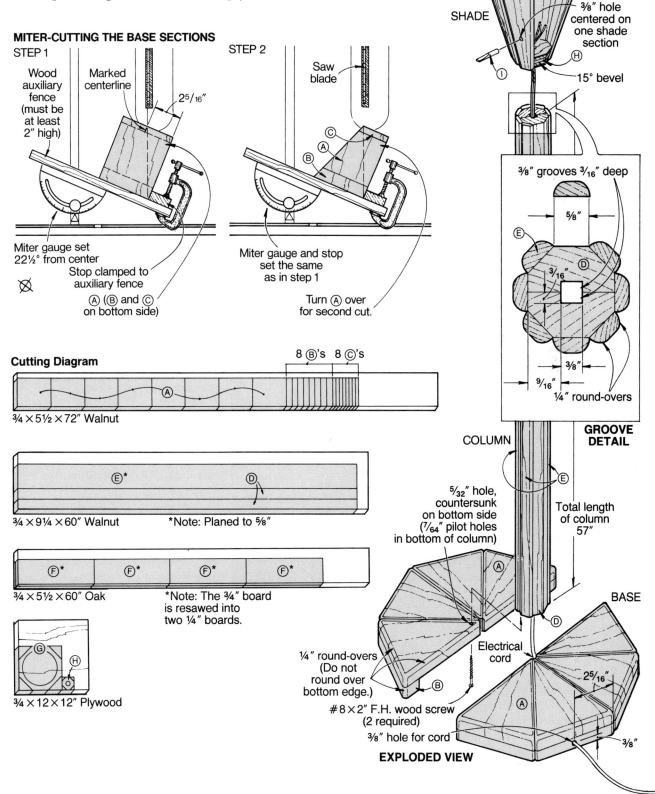

MITER-CUTTING THE BASE SECTIONS

STEP 1

Wood auxiliary fence (must be at least 2" high)

Marked centerline

2⁵⁄₁₆"

Miter gauge set 22½° from center

Stop clamped to auxiliary fence

Ⓐ (Ⓑ and Ⓒ on bottom side)

STEP 2

Saw blade

Ⓒ
Ⓐ
Ⓑ

Miter gauge and stop set the same as in step 1

Turn Ⓐ over for second cut.

Cutting Diagram

8 Ⓑ's   8 Ⓒ's

Ⓐ

¾ × 5½ × 72" Walnut

Ⓔ*   Ⓓ

¾ × 9¼ × 60" Walnut   *Note: Planed to ⅝"

Ⓕ*   Ⓕ*   Ⓕ*   Ⓕ*

¾ × 5½ × 60" Oak   *Note: The ¾" board is resawed into two ¼" boards.

Ⓖ
Ⓗ

¾ × 12 × 12" Plywood

SHADE

Ⓕ

15° bevel

¼" round-overs

⅜" hole centered on one shade section

Ⓗ

15° bevel

Ⓘ

⅜" grooves ³⁄₁₆" deep

⅝"

Ⓔ
Ⓓ

³⁄₁₆"

⅜"

⁹⁄₁₆"

¼" round-overs

GROOVE DETAIL

COLUMN

Ⓔ

⁵⁄₃₂" hole, countersunk on bottom side (⁷⁄₆₄" pilot holes in bottom of column)

Total length of column 57"

BASE

Ⓐ
Ⓓ

Electrical cord

¼" round-overs (Do not round over bottom edge.)

Ⓑ

#8 × 2" F.H. wood screw (2 required)

⅜" hole for cord

2⁵⁄₁₆"

Ⓐ

⅜"

EXPLODED VIEW

TORCHÈRE FLOOR LAMP
continued

with waxed paper as shown in photo A, *below.* Remove the excess glue, especially that near the round-overs. Repeat with the other four base sections.

7. Hold the two base half assemblies together; joint the mating edges if necessary. If you need to machine for a flush joint, remember to rerout a round-over and sand the jointed edges. Glue and hold the half sections together (we positioned the half assemblies on the plywood and held the pieces together with partially driven nails).

8. Using a sharp chisel, pry parts C from the lamp base.

9. Drill a ⅜" cord access hole, centered in the *end* of one base section where shown on the Exploded View Drawing, page 67. Now drill a ⅜" cord access hole through the *top center* of the base where shown.

Form the column pieces

1. Cut two pieces of ¾"-thick walnut to 1⅝ × 58" for the laminated column core (D).

2. Cut or rout a ⅜" groove ³⁄₁₆" deep, centered along one face of each piece of walnut. (See the Groove Detail accompanying the Exploded View Drawing.)

3. Glue and clamp the column pieces together groove to groove with the ends and edges flush. Later, scrape off the excess glue. Now plane the joined edges only; you'll want the laminated column core (D) to be 1½" square.

4. Position your tablesaw rip fence, and tilt the blade where shown on the drawing at *top right.* Bevel-rip each corner of the column core where shown on the drawing. Measure the width of all eight faces of the column core; you want each face to measure ⅝". Recut if necessary.

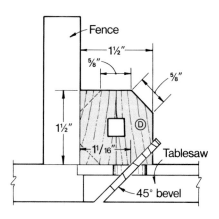

5. Cut a piece of ¾"-thick walnut to 4" wide by 58" long. Plane the piece to ⅝" thick. You want the board *thickness* to equal the *width* of each face (⅝") on the column core. (We reduced the thickness on our jointer; use a planer if you have one.) Position the fence on your tablesaw ¼" from the inside edge of the blade, and cut eight strips (E) from the walnut board, using a pushstick for safety. Each strip should measure ¼ × ⅝ × 58".

6. Chuck a ¼" round-over bit into your table-mounted router. Because the strips are too thin for the bit's bearing to be effective, position the fence and rout a ¼" round-over along the two outside faces of each strip. Finish-sand each strip.

Attach the strips to the column core

1. Position the strips around the column core, holding the strips in place with several rubber bands. Wrap loops of masking tape around the column (we wrapped six loops around the column, spacing the loops about 8" apart). Moving in a straight line down the column, cut each loop of masking tape once with a utility knife.

2. Remove the rubber bands, and unroll the tambourlike strip assembly. Using a small brush, apply an even coat   *continued*

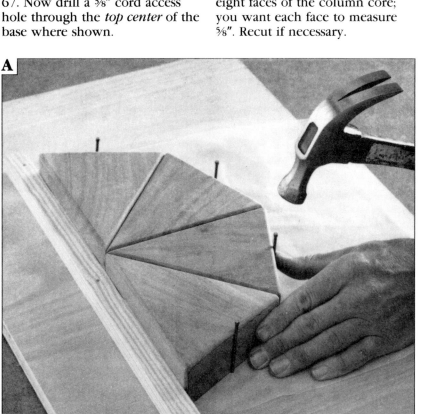

Glue four walnut base pieces together and hold in place against a straightedge with nails until the glue dries.

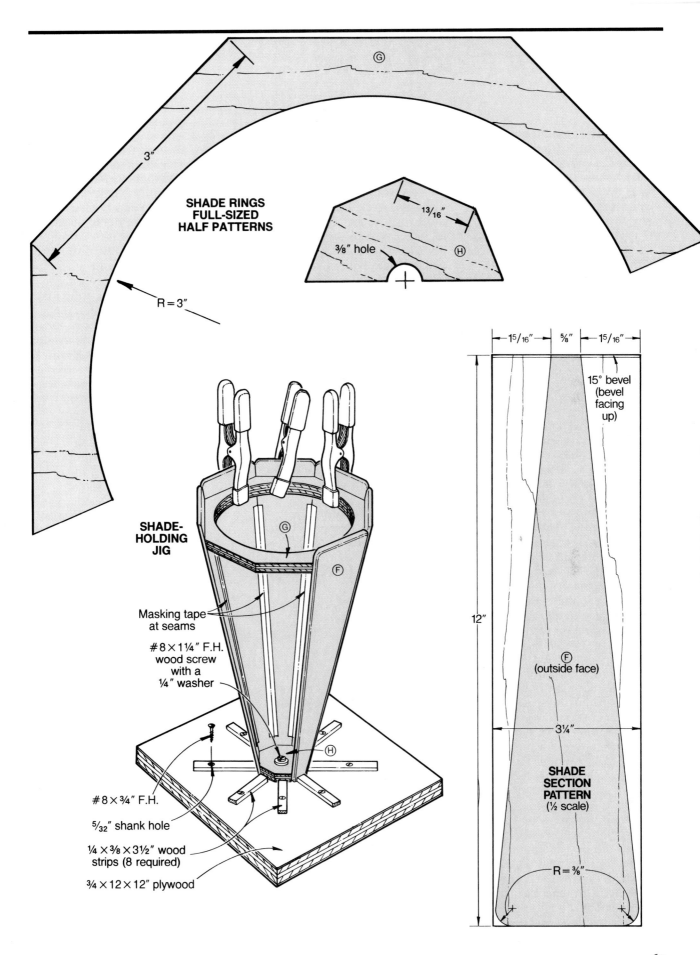

**SHADE RINGS
FULL-SIZED
HALF PATTERNS**

3"

R = 3"

G

13/16"

3/8" hole

H

**SHADE-
HOLDING
JIG**

G

F

Masking tape
at seams

#8 × 1¼" F.H.
wood screw
with a
¼" washer

H

#8 × ¾" F.H.

⁵/₃₂" shank hole

¼ × ⅜ × 3½" wood
strips (8 required)

¾ × 12 × 12" plywood

1⁵/₁₆"   ⅝"   1⁵/₁₆"

15° bevel
(bevel
facing
up)

12"

F
(outside face)

3¼"

**SHADE
SECTION
PATTERN**
(½ scale)

R = ⅜"

TORCHÈRE FLOOR LAMP
continued

of glue to the column core (D). Wrap the taped-together strips around the column core and hold in place with several large rubber bands. (We used a few spring clamps to help hold some unruly strips firmly in place.) Remove the tape, and immediately wipe the excess glue from the crevices with a damp cloth.

3. After the glue dries, remove the rubber bands. Then crosscut both ends of the column for a 57″ finished length.

Machine the shade pieces

1. Cut eight pieces of ½″ or ¾″ oak to 4″ wide by 13″ long for the shade sections (F). Plane or resaw each piece to ¼″ thick.

2. Tilt your saw blade 15° from center, set a stop, and bevel-cut the bottom end of each shade section for a 12″ finished length.

3. Using double-faced tape, adhere the pieces face-to-face, with the edges and ends flush. Referring to the Shade Section Pattern, page 69, transfer the shade pattern outline to the top oak piece. Bandsaw the stacked sections to shape. With the pieces still taped together, sand or joint the cut edges along the two sides. (When cutting the stacked pieces to shape, we cut slightly outside the marked line. Then we jointed to the line for perfectly straight edges.) Remove the double-faced tape to separate the shade pieces.

4. Back at your router table, rout a ¼″ round-over along the sides and top edge of the outside face (the same face as the bevel) of each shade section. Do not rout the previously beveled end or the two ⅜″-radiused corners. (We stood the pieces on edge and used a fence for support when routing.) Sand a round-over on the unrouted top two corners of each shade section, and then finish-sand each shade section smooth.

5. Using carbon paper, transfer the Full-Sized Half Patterns of the top ring (G) and the bottom ring (H), including the centerpoint of (H)(see page 69). Using a jigsaw, or with a circle cutter mounted to the drill press, cut the 6″-diameter hole in the center of the top ring. Drill a ⅜″ hole in the center of the bottom ring.

6. Tilt your bandsaw table 15° from center, and cut the perimeter of each of the two rings to shape.

7. Cut a 1⅝″ length of ¼″ walnut dowel for the switch knob (I). Hold the piece upright in a handscrew clamp, and drill a ³⁄₃₂″ hole ¼″ deep, centered into one end of the knob. Referring to the Knob Detail accompanying the Shade Section View Drawing, *opposite,* shape the opposite end of the knob on a belt sander. Set the knob aside for now.

Assemble the shade

1. Cut the pieces for a shade-holding jig (see page 69).

2. With the routed edges facing down, position the shade sections side by side. Tape the sections together (see photo B, *below*).

3. Position the shade assembly around the top and bottom rings, and tape together the remaining shade joint. The bottom of the bottom ring should be flush with the bottom of the shade assembly. Sand the beveled edges of the rings, if necessary for a snug fit. (The rings shouldn't force the taped joints apart.) Remove the tape from the areas on the inside of the shade that mate with the shade rings.

4. Remove the rings from the shade interior, and screw the bottom ring to the holding jig. Apply glue or epoxy to the beveled edges of each ring. Position the shade assembly around the bottom ring and position the top ring in place where shown on the Shade-Holding Jig Drawing. While you hold the shade upright, have a helper screw the wood strips in

B

Using masking tape, tape the oak shade sections tightly together with the top and bottom edges flush.

place to hold each section firmly against one beveled face of the bottom ring. Hold the top ring in place with spring clamps. After the glue dries, remove the strips and remaining masking tape. Unscrew the small ring from the holding jig.

Complete the assembly

1. To mount the column to the base, start by cutting a 5″ length of ⅜″ dowel. Stick the dowel 3″ into the bottom end of the column. Now stick the doweled end of the column into the ⅜″ hole in the center of the base. From the bottom side of the base, drill a pair of shank and pilot holes. Then screw and epoxy the column to the base, *checking that the column is square to the base.* Remove the ⅜″ dowel before the epoxy sets. Immediately wipe off any excess epoxy.

2. Thread the brass socket cap onto the top end of the threaded nipple. (See the Shade Section View Drawing, *right,* for help with the electrical wiring terminology we're using.) Tighten the setscrew.

3. Thread the nipple assembly through the hole in the small ring (H) until the bottom of the socket cap rests on the top face of the small ring (H).

4. Place the shade assembly on top of the column. Thread the exposed end of the nipple into the square hole in the small ring of the column. Align the joints of the shade sections with those of the column. Sand the bottom of the shade and top of the column flush, if necessary. Make a small reference mark so you can later realign the shade to the column. Now remove the shade from the column.

5. To join the shade to the column, apply epoxy to the bottom surface of the bottom ring and to the exposed portion of the threaded nipple. Position the shade on the column, realigning the joints and reference mark. Immediately remove any excess epoxy that squeezes out.

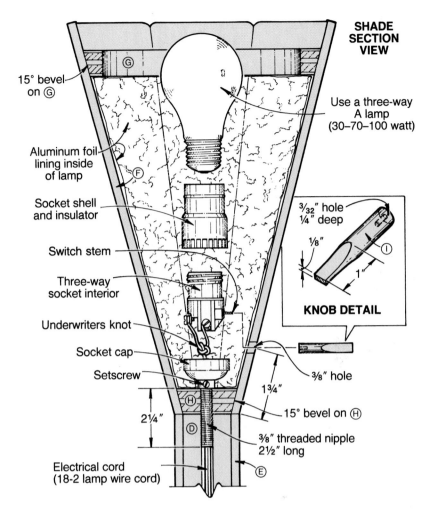

SHADE SECTION VIEW

15° bevel on Ⓖ

Aluminum foil lining inside of lamp

Socket shell and insulator

Switch stem

Three-way socket interior

Underwriters knot

Socket cap

Setscrew

2¼″

Electrical cord (18-2 lamp wire cord)

Use a three-way A lamp (30–70–100 watt)

3/32″ hole ¼″ deep

⅛″

1″

Ⓘ

KNOB DETAIL

⅜″ hole

1¾″

15° bevel on Ⓗ

⅜″ threaded nipple 2½″ long

6. Finish-sand the entire project (don't forget to sand away the reference mark). Apply a clear finish to the lamp and to the switch knob.

7. Fish the cord down through the socket cap and column, and through the holes in the base. Split the top 3″ of the cord, bare the ends, and tie an Underwriters knot above the socket cap. Wire the ends to the three-way socket. Push the socket into the socket cap. (To prevent the cord from doubling up in the column, you'll need to tug slightly on the bottom end of the cord when pushing the socket into the socket cap.) Attach a male end to the bottom end of the cord.

8. Carefully mark the knob-hole location on the outside of the shade assembly (see the Shade Section View and Exploded View

drawings for location). With the lamp standing upright, hold your drill level with the floor, and drill a ⅜″ hole into the shade for the switch knob (I).

9. Epoxy the switch knob onto the switch stem. Line the shade with aluminum foil. (The aluminum foil helps reflect light and radiate heat.) Install a three-way A lamp (30–70–100 watt).

Buying Guide

• **Electrical-supplies kit.** ⅜″ threaded nipple 2½″ long, light-bulb socket with 3-way switch, 12′ length of 18–2 lamp-wire cord, male end for cord. Kit no. WD37071. For current price, contact Albright Lighting, 3029 Ingersoll Ave., Des Moines, IA 50312.

CHIPPENDALE WALL MIRROR

In the 18th century, only the wealthy could afford to import mirrors (or looking glasses as they were called) from England. To accent these mirrors' beauty, colonial craftsmen built frames similar to the one shown here—a simplified version of a Chippendale-period (1750–1779) frame.

Form the frame

1. Cut the mirror-frame stiles (A), bottom rail (B), and top rail (C) to the sizes listed in the Bill of Materials. (We edge-joined narrower stock to make the wide top and bottom rails.)

2. Cut or rout a ⅜" rabbet ⅜" deep along the back inside edge of all four frame members. Now machine the same-size rabbets along both ends of the top and bottom rails where shown on the Frame Assembly Drawing, *opposite, center left.* (We test-cut scrap stock first to ensure the surfaces would be flush when the rabbeted pieces were held together.)

3. Glue and clamp the frame members together, checking to be sure they're square.

4. Using the drawing *below* for reference, lay out the angled top edges. Referring to the Full-Sized Pediment Half Pattern, *opposite, bottom left,* mark the top center of the top rail (C). *continued*

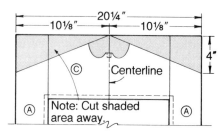

Bill of Materials					
Part	Finished Size			Mat.	Qty.
	T	W	L		
A stile	¾″	3½″	38″	O	2
B bottom rail	¾″	8″	14″	O	1
C top rail	¾″	6¾″	14″	O	1
D shelf	¾″	4″	16¾″	O	1
E support	¾″	3″	3⅛″	O	1
F pediment top	¾″	1½″	10¼″	O	2
G finial	1½″	1½″	3½″	LO	1
H back	⅛″	13⅞″	23⅞″	PLY	1

Material Key: O—oak, LO—laminated oak, PLY—plywood.
Supplies: 4—#8 × 1½″ flathead wood screws, 4—#8 × 1″ flathead wood screws, 2—# 10 × 2″ flathead wood screws, ⅛″ mirror, hotmelt adhesive, stain, finish.

EXPLODED VIEW

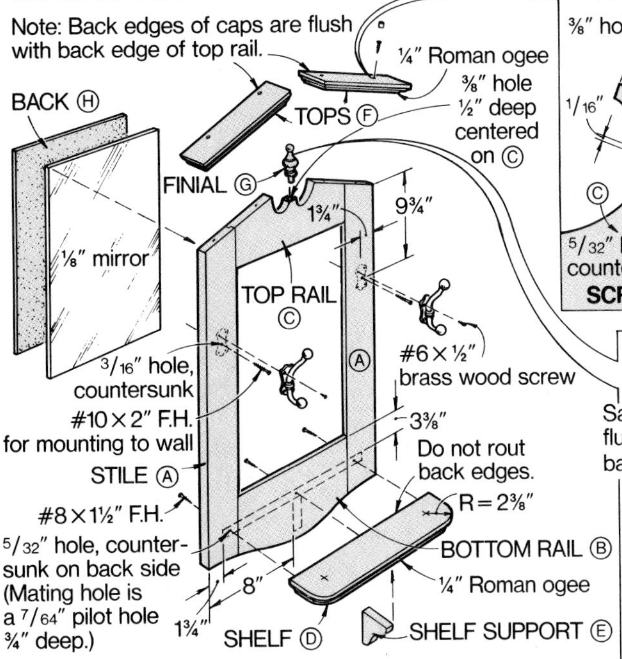

Note: Back edges of caps are flush with back edge of top rail.
BACK Ⓗ
TOPS Ⓕ
¼″ Roman ogee
⅜″ hole ½″ deep centered on Ⓒ
FINIAL Ⓖ
1¾″
9¾″
⅛″ mirror
TOP RAIL Ⓒ
Ⓐ
#6 × ½″ brass wood screw
³⁄₁₆″ hole, countersunk
#10 × 2″ F.H. for mounting to wall
3⅜″
Do not rout back edges.
STILE Ⓐ
R = 2⅜″
#8 × 1½″ F.H.
⁵⁄₃₂″ hole, countersunk on back side (Mating hole is a ⁷⁄₆₄″ pilot hole ¾″ deep.)
BOTTOM RAIL Ⓑ
8″
¼″ Roman ogee
1¾″
SHELF Ⓓ
SHELF SUPPORT Ⓔ

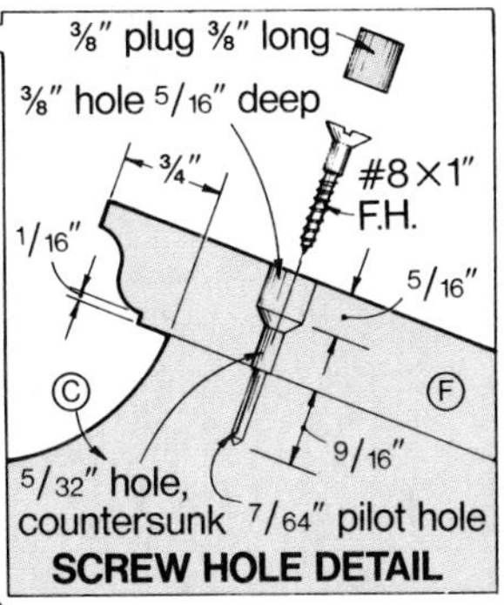

⅜″ plug ⅜″ long
⅜″ hole ⁵⁄₁₆″ deep
¾″
#8 × 1″ F.H.
¹⁄₁₆″
⁵⁄₁₆″
Ⓒ
Ⓕ
⁹⁄₁₆″
⁵⁄₃₂″ hole, countersunk
⁷⁄₆₄″ pilot hole
SCREW HOLE DETAIL

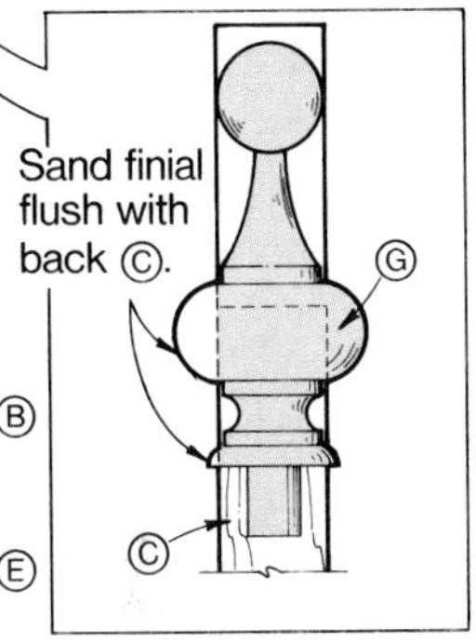

Sand finial flush with back Ⓒ.
Ⓖ
Ⓒ

FRAME ASSEMBLY
(View from back side)

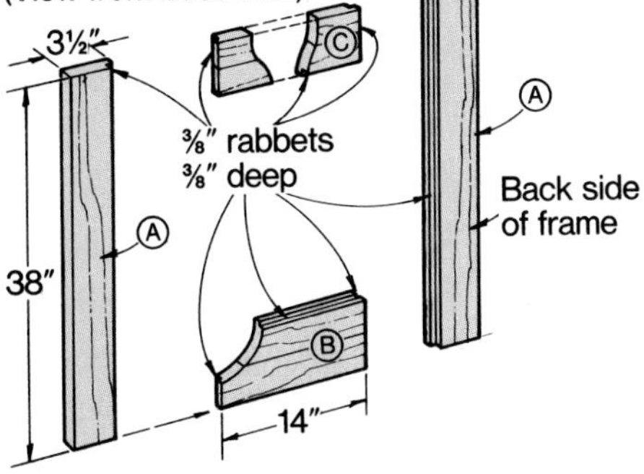

3½″
3½″
Ⓒ
⅜″ rabbets ⅜″ deep
Ⓐ
Ⓐ
Back side of frame
38″
Ⓑ
14″

Cutting Diagram
Note: Glue and clamp two pieces of ¾″ stock to form the finial turning square. Ⓖ

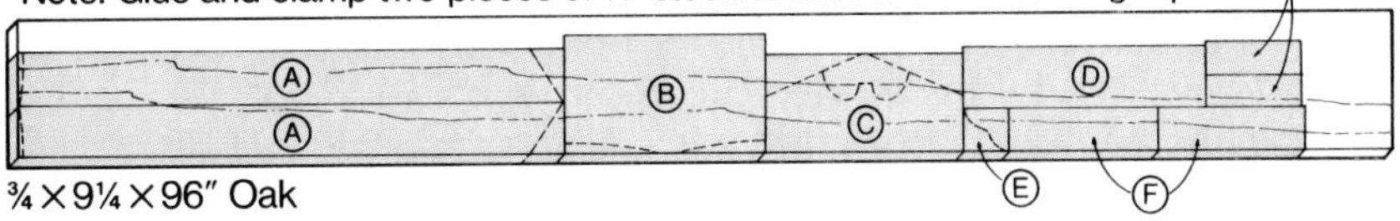

Ⓐ
Ⓐ
Ⓑ
Ⓒ
Ⓓ
Ⓔ
Ⓕ
¾ × 9¼ × 96″ Oak

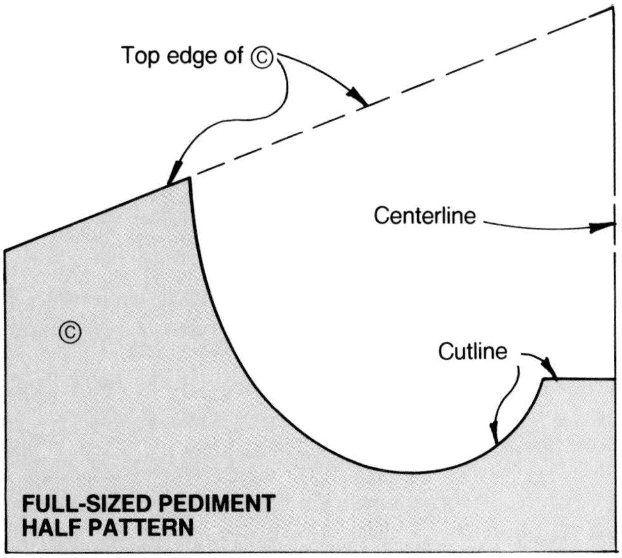

Top edge of Ⓒ
Centerline
Ⓒ
Cutline
FULL-SIZED PEDIMENT HALF PATTERN

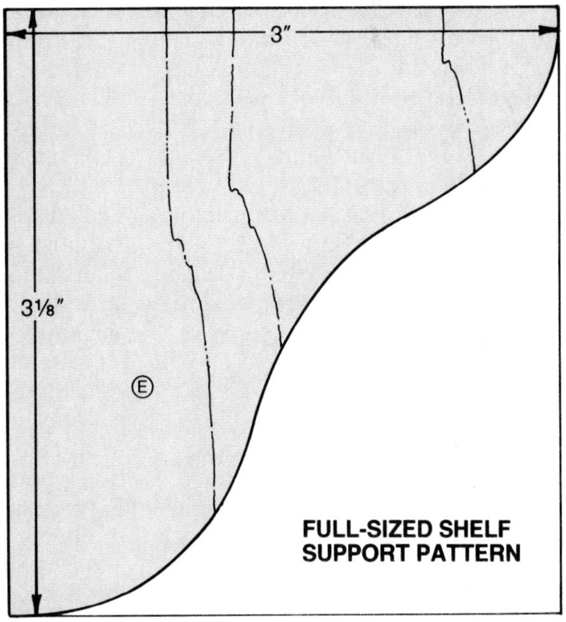

3″
3⅛″
Ⓔ
FULL-SIZED SHELF SUPPORT PATTERN

CHIPPENDALE WALL MIRROR
continued

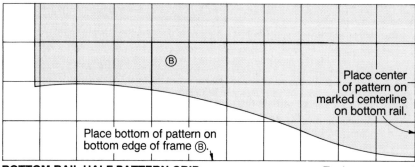

Place bottom of pattern on bottom edge of frame Ⓑ.

Place center of pattern on marked centerline on bottom rail.

BOTTOM RAIL HALF PATTERN GRID   Each square = 1″

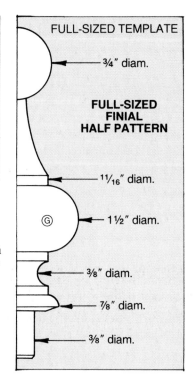

FULL-SIZED TEMPLATE

¾″ diam.

FULL-SIZED FINIAL HALF PATTERN

Ⓖ

¹¹⁄₁₆″ diam.

1½″ diam.

⅜″ diam.

⅞″ diam.

⅜″ diam.

5. Mark a centerline across the bottom rail (B). You'll use this line in the next step to position the template.

6. To enlarge the grid pattern for the bottom rail, cut a piece of heavy paper to 3×11″ and draw a 1″ grid on the paper. Referring to the Bottom Rail Half Pattern Grid, *above,* lay out the bottom-rail outline on the marked grid. To do this, mark the points where the pattern outline crosses each grid line. Finally, draw lines to connect the points. Cut the paper pattern to shape, align the inside edge with the marked centerline, and mark the shape of the frame bottom (you'll have to do this twice to mark both ends).

7. Bandsaw the frame top (pediment) and bottom to shape, and sand the cut edges to remove the saw marks. (We used a finish sander to remove the marks along the flat surfaces, and a drum sander to sand the curves.)

8. Drill a ³⁄₁₆″ hole in each stile (A) where located on the Exploded View Drawing, page 73. You'll use these holes later when attaching the mirror frame to the wall.

9. Center a coat hook over each of the mounting holes you drilled in the previous step. (See the Buying Guide for our source of hooks.) The coat hooks hide the

mounting screws after the mirror has been hung. Using the holes in the coat hook as guides, drill four pilot holes in each stile. Do not attach the coat hooks; you'll fasten them after hanging the completed frame on the wall.

Construct the shelf/support assembly

1. Cut the shelf (D) to 4×16¾″ from ¾″ stock. Mark a 2⅜″ radius on the front corners, cut the corners to shape, then sand them.

2. Rout a ¼″ Roman ogee along the front and sides of the shelf. See the Screw Hole Detail, page 73, for ogee-shape reference.

3. Cut a piece of ¾″-thick stock to 3×3⅛″ for the shelf support (E). Transfer the Full-Sized Shelf Support Pattern, page 73, to the blank with carbon paper or by adhering a photocopy. Bandsaw the support to shape. Sand the support smooth.

4. Mark the centerpoints for the support and shelf holes on the front face of the mirror frame. For hole centerpoints, see the Exploded View Drawing. Drill the holes.

5. Tape the shelf, centered over the holes just drilled, to the front of the mirror frame. Working from the back of the frame, and

using the holes as guides, drill pilot holes into the back of the shelf. Screw the shelf in place. Now center the shelf support under the shelf, and drill a pilot hole into it. Remove the shelf from the mirror frame.

Cut the pediment tops and turn the finial

1. Cut the pediment tops (F) to size. Next, rout a ¼″ Roman ogee along the bottom face of the front and side edges.

2. Drill and counterbore two mounting holes in each pediment top where shown on the Exploded View Drawing and to the sizes shown on the Screw Hole Detail.

3. With a portable hand drill, carefully drill a ⅜″ hole ½″ deep centered in the top of the top rail (C) for the finial.

4. Mount a 1½″ turning square 8″ long between centers on the

continued

lathe for the finial (G). If you don't have stock this size, laminate together two pieces of ¾"-thick stock.

5. Transfer the Full-Sized Finial Half Pattern, *opposite,* to poster board. Cut the template to shape. Using the template as a guide, turn the finial to shape as shown in photo A, *right.* (We used a small gouge and skew to shape the oak finial.) Being careful not to change the shape of the finial, sand it smooth with the lathe running at about 1,250 rpm. Using a parting tool, part it from the lathe. Sand the top ball-shaped portion of the finial.

6. Belt-sand the back of the finial. When mounted in the hole in the top rail, the back of the finial should be flush with the back of the mirror frame.

7. Glue the turned finial in place. Glue and screw the pediment tops in position. Cut plugs and fill the counterbores in the top surface of the pediment tops. Sand the plugs flush. Finish-sand all the parts.

8. Glue and screw the shelf and shelf support in place. Immediately wipe off any excess glue with a damp rag.

Add the finish, mirror, back, and then hang

1. Stain the assembly and apply at least two coats of clear finish.

2. Take the oak frame to a glass shop and have a mirror cut to the size of the opening *less ⅛" in length and width* to allow for contraction of the frame. Our rabbeted opening measures 14×24"; we cut our mirror and hardboard back to 13⅞×23⅞".

3. Cut the back (H) to size from plywood or hardboard, and secure it in place with hotmelt

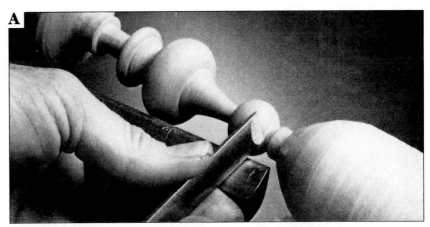
Shape the finial with a skew chisel.

Fasten the plywood back with hotmelt adhesive.

adhesive as shown in photo B, *above.* The hotmelt holds the back and mirror firmly in place, yet allows the frame to expand and contract.

4. Attach the coat hooks to the oak frame, then hang the frame on the wall.

Buying Guide
• **Coat hooks.** Two brass and porcelain coat hooks, catalog no. 64000. For current price, contact Armor Products, P.O. Box 445, East Northport, NY 11731. Or call 516/462-6228.

RACKS

*Rack 'em up! If you're looking for a place to stow
magazines, wine bottles and stemware, fishing rods, kids'
clothes, too-attractive-to-hide-away quilts, or coats that
never seem to make it to a closet, this final group of
projects will help get your household organized once and
for all.*

OAK MAGAZINE RACK

Looking for a project to test your skills in joinery? The magazine rack shown *opposite* features a center-lap joint that not only crosses at an oblique angle, but is tapered to boot! It begs to be cut by hand, and we'll show you how.

Note: You'll need some ½" oak for this project. You can either resaw or plane thicker stock to the correct thickness or special-order it.

Form the end panels

1. Cut the end panels (A) to a rectangular size of 10 × 12". (We edge-joined three boards for each end panel.)

2. Using double-faced tape, stick the two end panels together, with the best faces facing out and the edges flush.

3. Draw a 1" grid pattern measuring 10 × 12" on a piece of paper. Using the right half of the End Panel Half Grid, page 78, as a guide, mark the points where the end-panel outline crosses each grid line to lay out the end panel on the gridded paper. Fold the paper in half and cut it to shape. Unfold the paper and lay out the screw-hole locations.

4. Apply spray adhesive to the back of the gridded paper, and stick it to the face of one of the end panels. Cut slightly outside the marked outline with a bandsaw, then *continued*

Bill of Materials

Part	Finished Size*			Mat.	Qty.
	T	W	L		
A* end panel	¾"	9¾"	11⅛"	O	2
B handle	½"	2"	14"	O	1
C divider	½"	2"	14"	O	1
D bottom	½"	6"	14"	O	1
E lower rail	½"	¾"	14"	O	2
F* curved rail	½"	see grid		O	4

*Parts marked with an * are cut larger initially, then trimmed to finished size. Please read the instructions before cutting.

Material Key: O—oak.
Supplies: paper for drawing grid, #6 × 1¼" flathead wood screws, double-faced tape, spray adhesive, stain, finish.

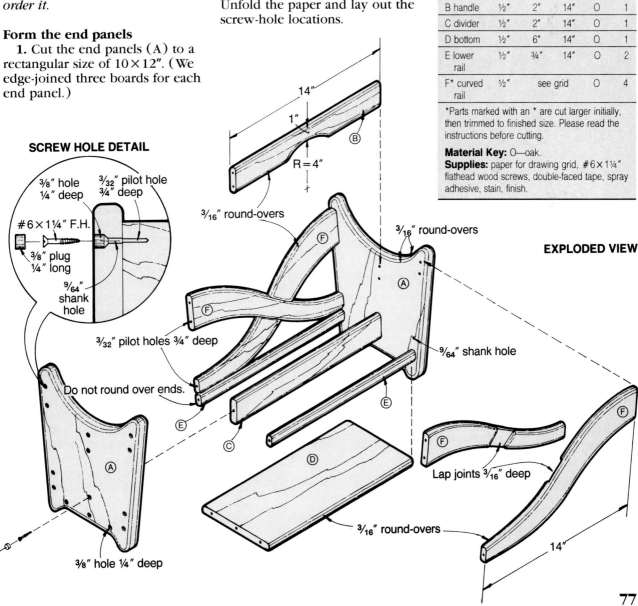

SCREW HOLE DETAIL

⅜" hole ¼" deep

³⁄₃₂" pilot hole ¾" deep

#6 × 1¼" F.H.

⅜" plug ¼" long

⁹⁄₆₄" shank hole

³⁄₁₆" round-overs

³⁄₁₆" round-overs

EXPLODED VIEW

³⁄₃₂" pilot holes ¾" deep

⁹⁄₆₄" shank hole

Do not round over ends.

Lap joints ³⁄₁₆" deep

³⁄₁₆" round-overs

14"

1"

R = 4"

14"

⅜" hole ¼" deep

OAK MAGAZINE RACK
continued

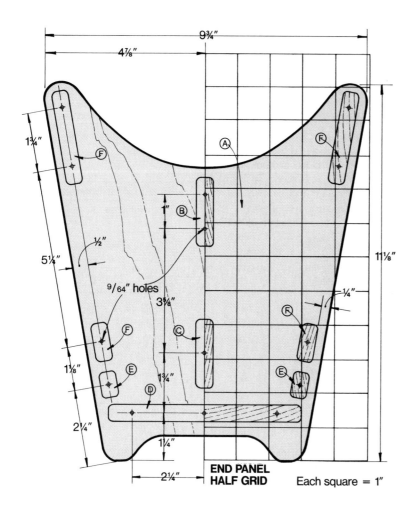

9¾"

4⅞"

1¾"

½"

5¼"

⁹⁄₆₄" holes

3⅜"

1⅛"

¼"

1¾"

2¼"

11⅛"

1¼"

2¼"

**END PANEL
HALF GRID**   Each square = 1"

Cutting Diagram

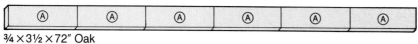

¾ × 3½ × 72" Oak

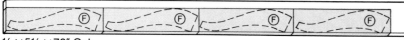

½ × 5½ × 72" Oak

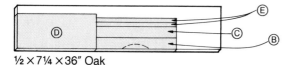

½ × 7¼ × 36" Oak

belt-sand the edges of both end panels down to the line for the finished shape.

5. With the ends still taped together, drill ⁹⁄₆₄" shank holes where marked, drilling completely through both end panels. (We placed a scrap board under the ends to keep chip-out to a minimum.)

6. Using the ⁹⁄₆₄" shank holes as guides, counterbore ⅜" holes ¼" deep for the plugs on each end panel (see the Screw Hole Detail accompanying the Exploded View Drawing, page 77). Now separate the end panels, and remove the double-faced tape. Then rout a ³⁄₁₆" round-over on all edges of both end panels.

Cut the handle, divider, bottom, and lower rails

Note: Parts B, C, D, E, and F are joined to the end panels using glued butt joints reinforced with wood screws. For a proper fit, make sure you cut all these parts to the same length.

1. Cut the handle (B), divider (C), bottom (D), and lower rails (E) to the sizes listed in the Bill of Materials, page 77, from ½" oak. (We ripped all the pieces first. Then we set a stop 14" from the blade of our radial-arm saw to ensure a consistent length.) Cut the center-radiused handgrip in the handle where shown on the Exploded View Drawing.

2. Locate the center of each end of the divider, bottom, and both lower rails, then drill a ³⁄₃₂" pilot hole ¾" deep in each. Locate and drill *one* ³⁄₃₂" hole in each end of the handle (the second hole on each end of the handle will be drilled later).

3. Rout a ³⁄₁₆" round-over along the edges, but *not* the ends, of the handle, divider, bottom, and both lower rails.

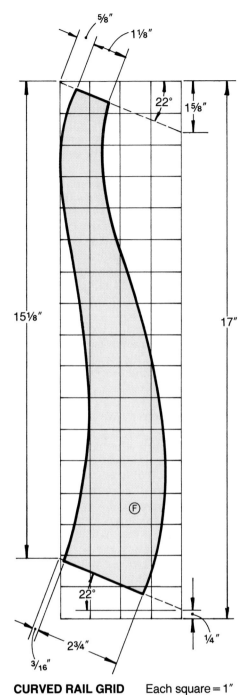

CURVED RAIL GRID   Each square = 1"

4. Make a trial assembly of the parts by screwing the handle, divider, bottom, and both lower rails between the end panels. Do *not* use glue.

5. Using a straightedge, align the handle with the divider. Using the ⁹⁄₆₄" shank holes previously drilled in the end panels as guides, drill the second set of ³⁄₃₂" holes in the handle

LAYING OUT THE LAP JOINTS

STEP 1. Hold rails together with a spring clamp.

STEP 2. Align both rail ends with square.

STEP 3. Mark location of lap joints on both pieces.

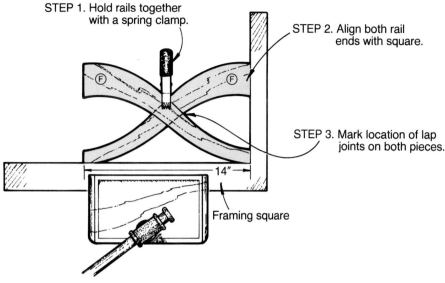

Framing square

ends. Square the bottom piece with the divider and handle, then drill the second set of holes in the bottom. Set the assembly aside. You will need it later to determine the length of the curved rails (F).

Fashion the curved rails

1. Cut four pieces of ½" oak 4 × 17". With a ruler and straightedge, lay out 1" squares on paper to form a pattern measuring 4 × 17". Using the Curved Rail Grid, *left*, as a guide, mark the points where the curved-rail outline crosses each grid line. Use a thin flexible scrap of wood to connect the points to form the curved lines. Use spray adhesive on the back of the pattern to attach it to one of the curved-rail blanks (F).

2. With the edges and ends flush, temporarily stick the four curved-rail pieces together with double-faced tape.

3. Set your radial-arm saw or tablesaw to cut 22° right of center, and trim the ends of the taped-together boards. Cut the curved rails to shape. Now sand the edges of the rails (but not ends) smooth. Remove the gridded paper.

4. Clamp the taped-together rails in a woodworker's vise with the narrow ends up and level. Drill a ³⁄₃₂" pilot hole ¾" deep, centered into the narrow end of each curved rail. Pull the rails apart and remove the tape. Then rout a ³⁄₁₆" round-over along the edges, but *not* the ends, of each curved rail.

5. To lay out the lap joint on the rails, start by clamping a framing square in your woodworker's vise. Then position paired rails as shown on the Laying Out the Lap Joints Drawing, *above*, so that one end of each pair is *flush* with the square, and opposite ends are exactly 14" apart. (Trim the curved rails at 22° if they are a bit too long. If they are too short, trim B, C, D, and E.) Use a spring clamp to hold the paired rails together after you have them properly aligned.

6. Use a sharp pencil to mark both curved rails where they overlap. Then separate the rails, and repeat for the other pair, keeping the paired rails together. To mark the depth of cut needed for each lap joint, measure and mark a line ³⁄₁₆" from the face on each curved rail   *continued*

OAK MAGAZINE RACK
continued

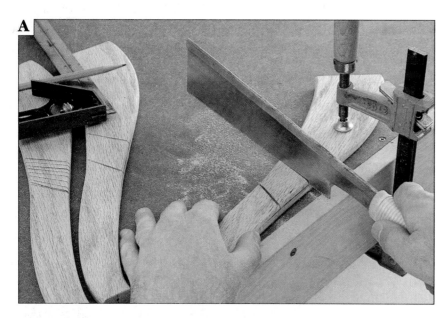

framing square to align the ends of the rail pairs. Now, before the glue on the curved rails sets, clamp them in position, centering the bottom ends over the ⁹⁄₆₄″ shank holes drilled earlier in the end panels. Screw the bottom end of each curved rail to the end panel, using spring clamps to hold them together at the lap joints. Using the shank holes in the end panels as guides, drill a pair of ³⁄₃₂″ holes in the upper ends of each curved rail.

Assemble the rack

1. Disassemble the rack by removing the screws. Sand all the pieces smooth; it's too difficult to finish-sand all the pieces after the rack is assembled.

2. Glue and screw all the parts to one end panel. (We applied a coat of glue to the end grain, waited a minute, then added a bit more.) When one end of the assembly is completed, attach the opposite end panel in the same manner. Scrape off all excess glue once a tough skin has formed, being careful not to mar the sanded surfaces.

3. With a ³⁄₈″ plug cutter, cut ⁵⁄₁₆″-long oak plugs. (We planed down a scrap piece of the ½″ oak to ⁵⁄₁₆″. Then we chucked the plug cutter in our drill press, clamped the scrap to the table, and proceeded to cut the plugs.) Glue the plugs in place with the grain of the plugs running the same direction as the grain of the end panels. Sand the plugs flush.

4. Sand all surfaces smooth. Apply the stain and finish of your choice to the magazine rack.

(we used a combination square and sharp pencil for this).

7. As shown in photo A, *top,* make the first two cuts ³⁄₁₆″ deep on the *inside* of the marked lap-joint lines. Then cut several more kerfs between the first two (the closer together the kerfs are, the easier the waste is to chisel out in the next step).

8. Chisel the waste between the lap lines, as shown in photo B, *above.* (You also could use a router fitted with a straight bit to make the recess.) Finish by taking finer cuts with the chisel, then touch up with a rasp, if necessary. Test-fit the pieces.

9. Glue both pairs of curved rails together, again using the

FREESTANDING WINE RACK

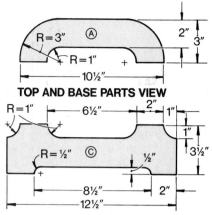

TOP AND BASE PARTS VIEW

base pieces as shown in photo A, *below.* Clamp these two pieces to your drill-press table, and bore the two 1″ holes and four 2″ holes where marked to form the radii. Repeat these operations on the other base.

Bore holes in the walnut base pieces with a Forstner bit to form the ½″- and 1″-radius curves.

To complete the curved cutouts, bandsaw between the drilled holes, using the saw's fence as a guide.

With room for eight bottles of your finest wine and just as many stemmed glasses, this freestanding unit makes exceptionally good use of a small amount of space. And guess what? It's a snap to build because the joinery can be easily accomplished with a doweling jig and dowel pins. Why not make several and treat friends or relatives with this special gift?

Form the end frames

1. For the two end frames, cut the top pieces (A), uprights (B), and bases (C) to the sizes listed in the Bill of Materials, page 82. Then, referring to the Top and Base Parts View Drawing, *top right,* mark the radii for all of the curves on the tops and bases.

2. Cut a piece of scrap that's at least as long as the base pieces (12½″). Now clamp the scrap to the bottom edge of one of the

3. With your bandsaw, cut straight lines between the holes to shape the bases as shown in photo B, *above.* *continued*

FREESTANDING WINE RACK
continued

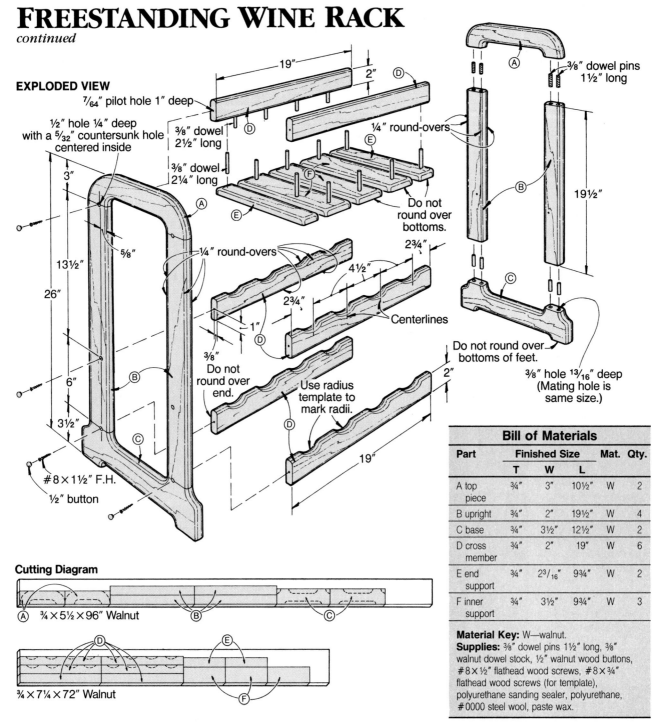

EXPLODED VIEW

$\frac{7}{64}$" pilot hole 1" deep

$\frac{1}{2}$" hole $\frac{1}{4}$" deep with a $\frac{5}{32}$" countersunk hole centered inside

3"

13½"

26"

6"

3½"

$\frac{5}{8}$"

$\frac{3}{8}$" dowel 2½" long

$\frac{3}{8}$" dowel 2¼" long

¼" round-overs

$\frac{3}{8}$"

Do not round over end.

Use radius template to mark radii.

19"

2"

2¾"

4½"

2¾"

1"

Centerlines

19"

2"

¼" round-overs

Do not round over bottoms.

$\frac{3}{8}$" dowel pins 1½" long

19½"

Do not round over bottoms of feet.

$\frac{3}{8}$" hole $\frac{13}{16}$" deep (Mating hole is same size.)

#8 × 1½" F.H.

½" button

Cutting Diagram

Ⓐ ¾ × 5½ × 96" Walnut   Ⓑ   Ⓒ

¾ × 7¼ × 72" Walnut

Ⓓ Ⓔ Ⓕ

Bill of Materials				
Part	Finished Size		Mat.	Qty.
	T	W	L	
A top piece	¾"	3"	10½"	W	2
B upright	¾"	2"	19½"	W	4
C base	¾"	3½"	12½"	W	2
D cross member	¾"	2"	19"	W	6
E end support	¾"	2³⁄₁₆"	9¾"	W	2
F inner support	¾"	3½"	9¾"	W	3

Material Key: W—walnut.
Supplies: ⅜" dowel pins 1½" long, ⅜" walnut dowel stock, ½" walnut wood buttons, #8 × ½" flathead wood screws, #8 × ¾" flathead wood screws (for template), polyurethane sanding sealer, polyurethane, #0000 steel wool, paste wax.

4. Repeat the boring and cutting process (steps 2 and 3) to shape both top pieces of the rack's end frames.

5. Dry-clamp the pieces (A, B, C) of each end frame together, and mark dowel-hole reference lines where dimensioned on the Locating the Dowel Holes Drawing, *opposite, top.* Remove the clamps after marking.

6. Using a doweling jig, drill ⅜" holes ¹³⁄₁₆" deep where marked on the end frame parts. Glue, dowel, and clamp each end frame together.

7. Using the dimensions and hole sizes on the Exploded View Drawing, *above,* drill six plug and shank holes in each end frame so you can attach the cross members (D) later.

8. Sand each end frame smooth (we used a 2"-diameter drum sander on the inside radii and a palm sander on the other surfaces). Now rout a ¼" round-over on all but the bottom edges of the feet of both end frames. Finish-sand each end frame.

Shape the bottle rests

1. Cut the four bottle rests and the two top cross members (D) to 2×19″. Mark diagonal lines on each *end* of each piece to find the center, and drill a ⁷⁄₆₄″ pilot hole 1″ deep at each of the centerpoints. (Be careful to keep the hole at a right angle to the surface being drilled.) Set aside the two top cross members; you'll use them later.

2. To mark the radii on the four bottle rests, first make the Radius Template, *below.* Mark centerlines on each bottle rest where dimensioned on the Exploded View Drawing. Align the centerline on the template with those on each bottle rest, and mark four radii on each bottle rest.

LOCATING THE DOWEL HOLES

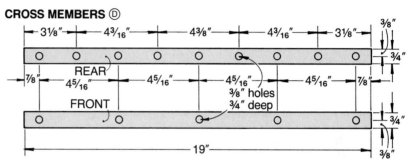

CROSS MEMBERS Ⓓ

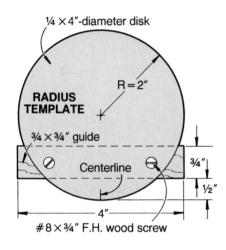

3. Cut the radii to shape on the bandsaw. Use a drum sander to sand the radii smooth. Then rout a ¼″ round-over along all edges, but not along the ends. Finish-sand the four bottle rests.

Build the stemware supports

1. Cut the two walnut end supports (E) and three inner supports (F) to size.

2. Using the Stemware Supports Drawing, *right,* mark the location of the dowel holes on each support. Drill a pair of ⅜″ holes ½″ deep in each support.

3. Rout a ¼″ round-over along the top edges of each support and

along all but the ends of the two remaining cross members (D). Sand the parts smooth.

4. Drill five holes in the front cross member and nine holes in the rear cross member, using the dimensions and hole size on the Cross Members Drawing, *above* (we drilled ours with a doweling jig).

5. Cut 10 pieces of ⅜″ walnut dowel stock to 2¼″ long and four pieces to 2½″ long.

6. Using the 2¼″-long dowels, glue and clamp the stemware assembly (D, E, F) together. Check that the supports are level

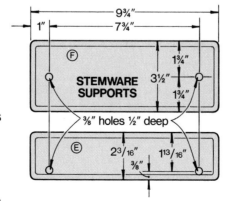

with each other and square the assembly. Sand a round-over on one edge of each of the four 2½″-long dowels. Glue the four dowels (rounded ends exposed) in the back cross member. These dowels prevent the glasses from sliding out the back.

Assemble the wine rack

1. Spread an even coat of glue on the ends of each cross member (D), and screw the bottle rests and stemware rack between the end frames. Wipe off any excess glue with a damp cloth. Glue ½″ wood buttons in the screw holes.

2. Stain and finish as desired. (We applied two coats of polyurethane sanding sealer and three coats of polyurethane, steel-wooling between coats. Next, we used the steel wool to apply a coat of Minwax paste finishing wax. Finally, we buffed the wax with a cloth.)

FISHING ROD RACK

We can report excellent fishing conditions for our anglin' friends: They're biting on this rod rack idea. In addition to looking like a million bucks, the rack untangles the rod-and-reel mess that bobs up at many homes between outings. And that's no fish story.

Start with the mounting boards

1. From ¾" walnut, cut the two mounting boards (A) to 4×24".

2. Mark a centerline the length of each board. Center a compass point on the marked line, and mark a 2" radius on the ends of each board. Cut the marked ends to shape and sand both boards.

3. Using the dimensions on the Upper Unit and Base Unit drawings, *opposite,* mark three centerpoints on the centerline of each mounting board for the ⁵⁄₃₂" holes. You'll use these holes later for mounting the rod holder (B) and butt-end support (E). Measure down ⅝" from the center of each *outside* centerpoint on the upper-unit mounting board and down ¾" on the base-unit mounting board, and mark a pair of centerpoints on each board. You'll use these holes later for mounting the assemblies to the wall. Drill a ⁵⁄₃₂" hole at each centerpoint and countersink where shown on the drawings.

4. Rout a ¼" cove along the front face of each mounting board. Sand both boards smooth.

Construct the rod holder and butt-end support

1. Cut a piece of ½"-thick walnut to 2×22¾". If you don't have any ½" stock, plane or resaw thicker stock.

2. Rip a 1¼"-wide strip from the ½" walnut for the rod holder

(B). Rip a strip ⅛" wide from the remaining piece for the top retainer strip (C). Repeat the process to rip a ⅛×23" bottom retainer strip (D) from the edge of a ¾"-thick board.

3. Follow steps 1 through 6 on the Forming the Rod Holder Drawing, *opposite, right,* to finish assembling the rod holder (B). (You'll do steps 7 and 8 later.)

4. Cut the butt-end support (E) to 2×23". Referring to the dimensions on the Base Unit Drawing, mark the dado locations. Cut the 1½" dadoes ⅜" deep. Wrap sandpaper around a ¾"-thick piece of scrapwood, and sand the dado bottoms.

5. Glue and clamp the ¾" retainer strip (D) to the front edge of the butt-end support. Mark and miter-cut the ends.

6. Sand the two mounting boards, the rod holder, and the butt-end support. Glue and screw the rod holder and butt-end support to the mounting boards.

Shape your fish

Note: If you prefer not to spend the time cutting and shaping the decorative fish, skip to the section titled "Finish the rack, hang it, and add the rods" to complete the rod rack.

1. Trace or photocopy the Full-Sized Front View Pattern, pages 86 and 87. Cut the pattern to shape.

2. Cut a piece of ¾" oak to 5×14" for the fish blank (F). With carbon paper, transfer the fish pattern and eye centerpoint to the oak. Cut the fish to shape, and cut *continued*

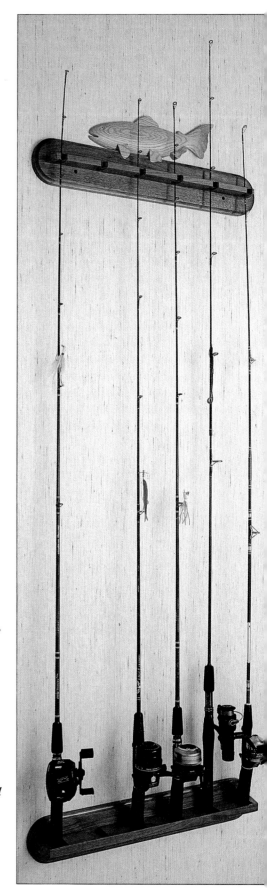

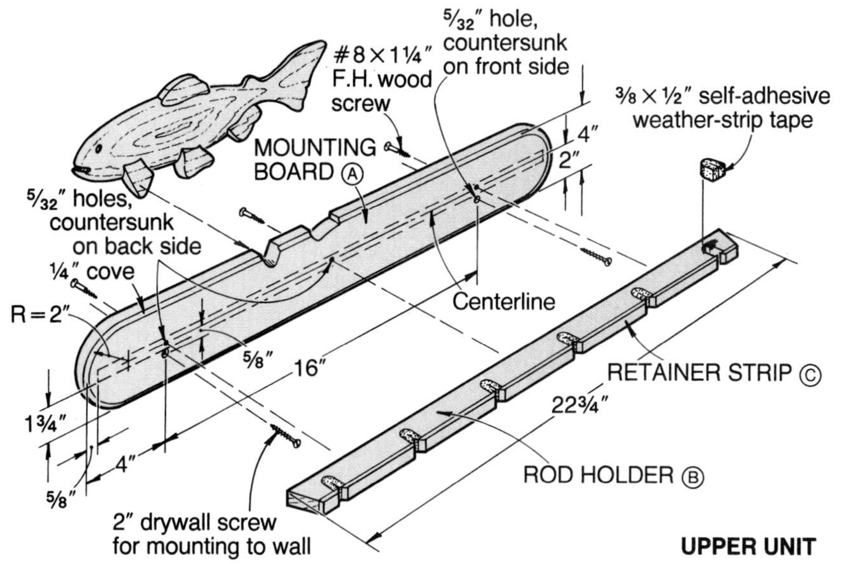
5/32" hole, countersunk on front side
#8×1¼" F.H. wood screw
3/8 × ½" self-adhesive weather-strip tape
MOUNTING BOARD Ⓐ
4"
2"
5/32" holes, countersunk on back side
¼" cove
Centerline
R=2"
5/8"
16"
RETAINER STRIP Ⓒ
22¾"
1¾"
4"
5/8"
ROD HOLDER Ⓑ
2" drywall screw for mounting to wall
UPPER UNIT

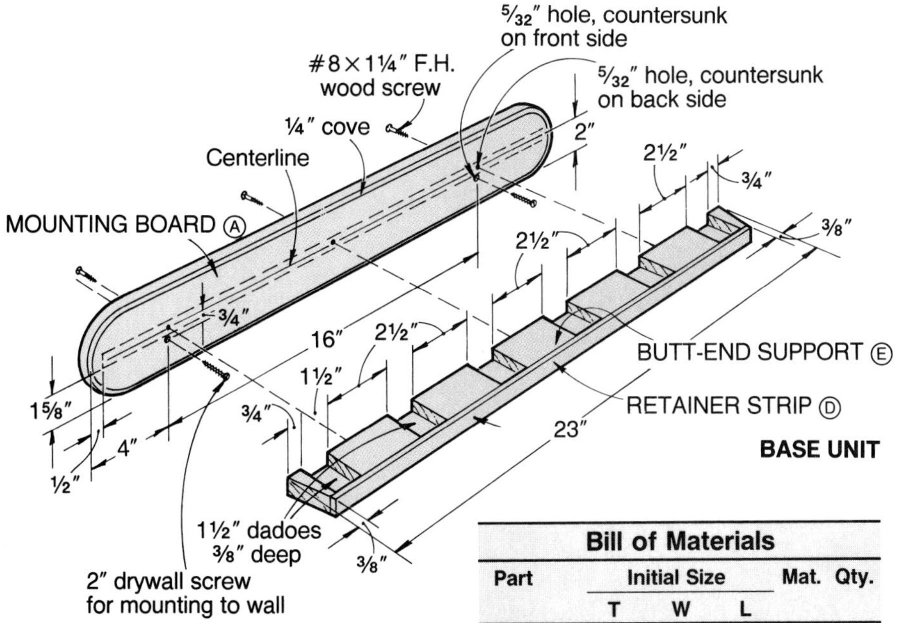
5/32" hole, countersunk on front side
#8×1¼" F.H. wood screw
5/32" hole, countersunk on back side
¼" cove
2"
Centerline
2½"
¾"
MOUNTING BOARD Ⓐ
3/8"
2½"
¾"
16"
2½"
BUTT-END SUPPORT Ⓔ
1½"
1⅝"
¾"
RETAINER STRIP Ⓓ
4"
23"
½"
BASE UNIT
1½" dadoes 3/8" deep
3/8"
2" drywall screw for mounting to wall

Cutting Diagram

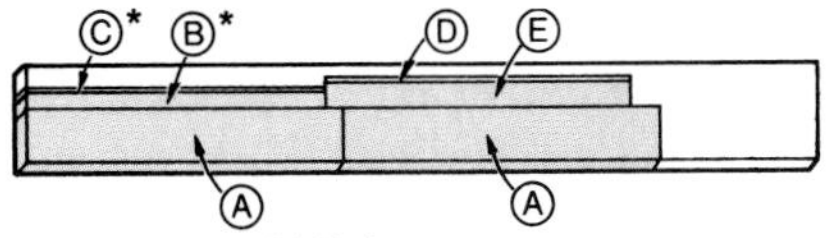
Ⓒ* Ⓑ* Ⓓ Ⓔ
Ⓐ Ⓐ

¾ × 7¼ × 72" Walnut
*Note: Plane or resaw Ⓑ and Ⓒ to ½".

Bill of Materials

Part	Initial Size T	W	L	Mat.	Qty.
A mounting board	¾"	4"	24"	W	2
B rod holder	½"	1¼"	22¾"	W	1
C retainer strip	⅛"	½"	22¾"	W	1
D retainer strip	⅛"	¾"	23"	W	1
E butt-end support	¾"	2"	23"	W	1
F fish blank	¾"	5"	14"	O	1

Material Key: W—walnut, O—oak.
Supplies: weather-strip tape with self-adhesive backing (the closed-cell tape we used measures ½" wide by ⅜" thick), #8 × 1¼" flathead wood screws, 2" drywall screws or toggle bolts, finish.

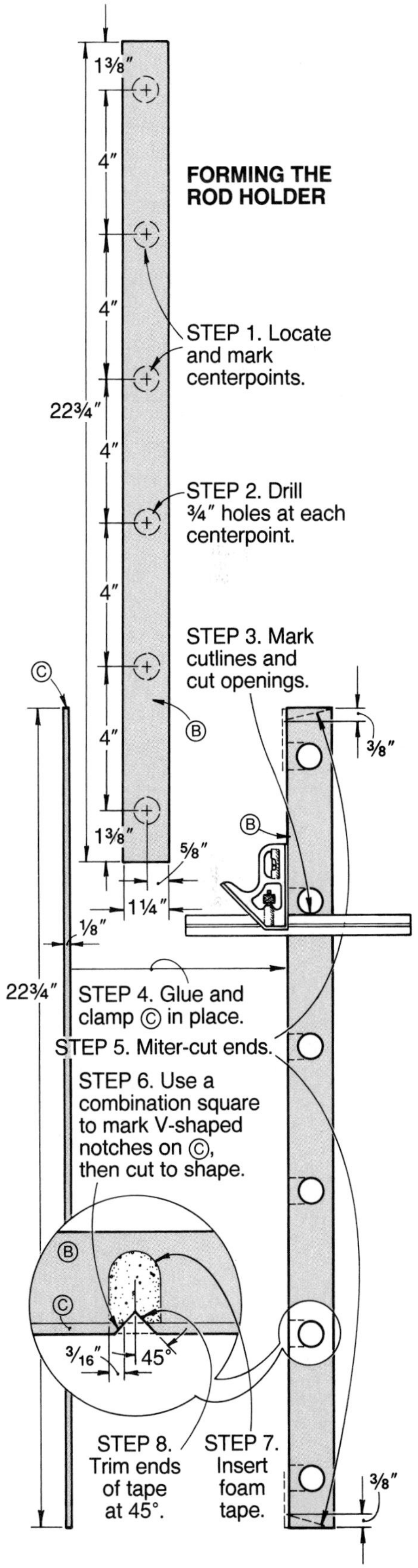
1⅜"
4"
FORMING THE ROD HOLDER
4"
STEP 1. Locate and mark centerpoints.
22¾"
4"
STEP 2. Drill ¾" holes at each centerpoint.
4"
STEP 3. Mark cutlines and cut openings.
Ⓒ
4"
Ⓑ
3/8"
1⅜"
Ⓑ
5/8"
1¼"
⅛"
22¾"
STEP 4. Glue and clamp Ⓒ in place.
STEP 5. Miter-cut ends.
STEP 6. Use a combination square to mark V-shaped notches on Ⓒ, then cut to shape.
Ⓑ
Ⓒ
3/16"
45°
STEP 8. Trim ends of tape at 45°.
STEP 7. Insert foam tape.
3/8"

FISHING ROD RACK
continued

around the outlines of the fins to separate the fins from the body. (We used a scrollsaw.) Cutting the fins from the body allows you to sand the fish body and fins separately.

3. Using a brad-point bit, drill a ⅜″ hole ¼″ deep for the fish's eye where marked.

4. Chuck a 60-grit drum sander into your drill press or portable drill. Referring to the Full-Sized Top View Pattern, *below*, and the photo at *right*, sand the fish body to shape. (The front end of a belt sander also works well.)

5. To make the back fin appear to be moving, sand the back side of the tail fin to the shape shown on the Full-Sized Top View Pattern.

6. As shown on the drawing *opposite*, position the fish body on a flat surface. Place each fin

into the recess from which it was cut. Mark a line from the bottom outside edge of the fins to the point where the fins meet the contoured-fish body. Draw another line across each fin as

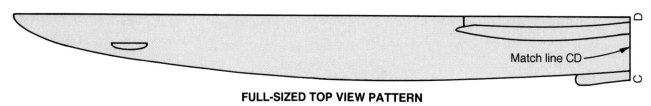

FULL-SIZED TOP VIEW PATTERN

Match line CD

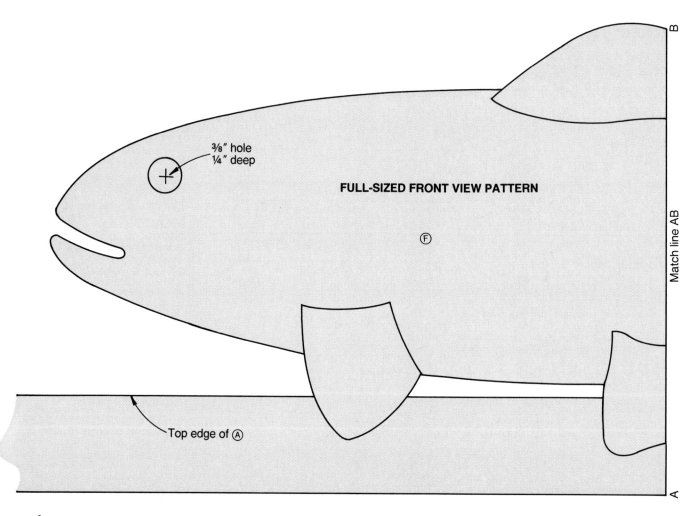

⅜″ hole
¼″ deep

FULL-SIZED FRONT VIEW PATTERN

Ⓕ

Top edge of Ⓐ

Match line AB

shown. Sand to the lines to shape the fins.

Mount the fish

1. Glue the fins into position against the fish body.

2. Position the fish over the top mounting board, center it between the ends, and trace the two fin patterns onto the top of the mounting board. See the Upper Unit Drawing, page 85, for reference. Cut away the material you just outlined on the mounting board. Glue the fish into place on the top of the board.

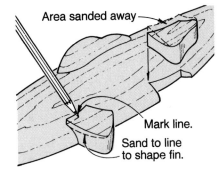

Area sanded away

Mark line.

Sand to line to shape fin.

Finish the rack, hang it, and add the rods

1. Finish-sand all the parts; then apply the finish of your choice. (We used several coats of polyurethane varnish.)

2. Cut six 2¾"-long pieces from ½"-wide weather-strip tape. Remove the paper backing, and insert the foam strips into the notches in the rod holder where shown in step 7 on the Forming the Rod Holder Drawing, page 85. Using a sharp razor blade, follow step 8 to cut the ends of the tape.

3. Use 2" drywall screws if you can hit a stud; if not, use toggle bolts to attach the upper and base units to the wall.

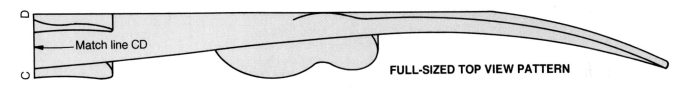

Match line CD

FULL-SIZED TOP VIEW PATTERN

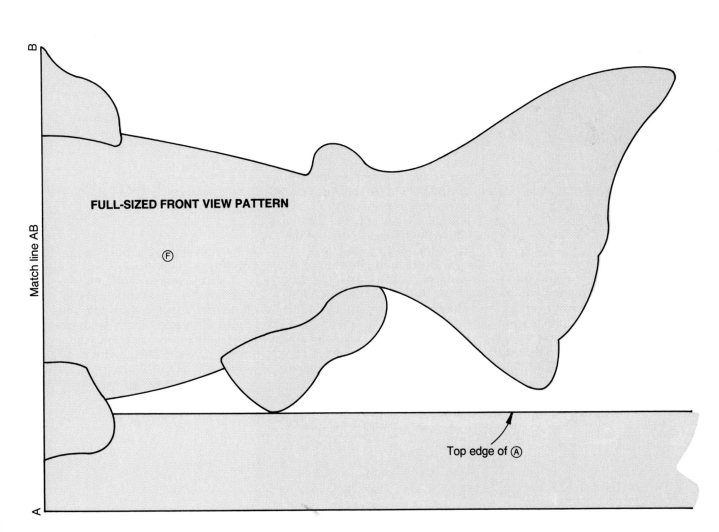

FULL-SIZED FRONT VIEW PATTERN

F

Match line AB

Top edge of Ⓐ

RABBIT CLOTHES RACK

J ust watch how your child's room changes after you hang this whimsical bunny on the wall. Who knows, pretty soon you may not even have to complain about a messy room.

1. Using the Full-Sized Front View Pattern, *opposite*, for reference, lay out on paper separate patterns for the head and upper body (A), nose (B), teeth (C), and one eyebrow (D). Mark the centerpoints for the two hanger dowels, eyes, and nostrils. Cut the patterns to shape.

2. Spray the back side of the paper patterns with spray adhesive. Adhere the head, nose, and eyebrow patterns to ¾"-thick stock (we used cedar) and the teeth to ¾" pine. Cut the pieces to shape. Use the nose piece (B) as a template to mark the second nose piece. Do the same with the teeth. Then cut the second nose and tooth pieces to shape.

3. Bandsaw the ¾"-thick eyebrow piece in half to form two thinner pieces (D). Glue and clamp the two nose pieces together.

4. Referring to the Side View Drawing, *right,* tilt your drill-press table 30° from center, and drill two ⅜" holes ½" deep for the hanging dowels in the head piece. Drill holes for the eyes and nose. Remove the paper patterns from the wood pieces. Drill two angled holes in the back of the head for hanging on a wall.

5. Drum-sand or cut the back surface of the teeth (C) to the shape shown on the Side View Drawing, *right.* Sand all the pieces smooth.

6. Glue the teeth to the bottom of and flush with the front center of the nose pieces. Later, clamp the nose-teeth assembly in a handscrew clamp, and bandsaw a ⅛"-deep kerf in the front edge.

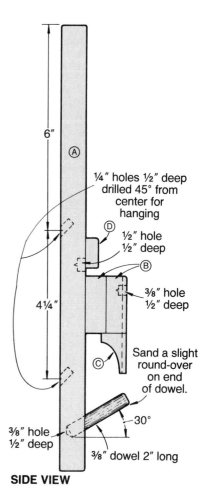

SIDE VIEW

Glue and clamp the nose and eyebrows to the head.

7. Cut to length, and glue two ⅜" dowels in the holes in the head and upper body. Apply the finish of your choice. (We used polyurethane varnish, but you might consider using paint to add some color.)

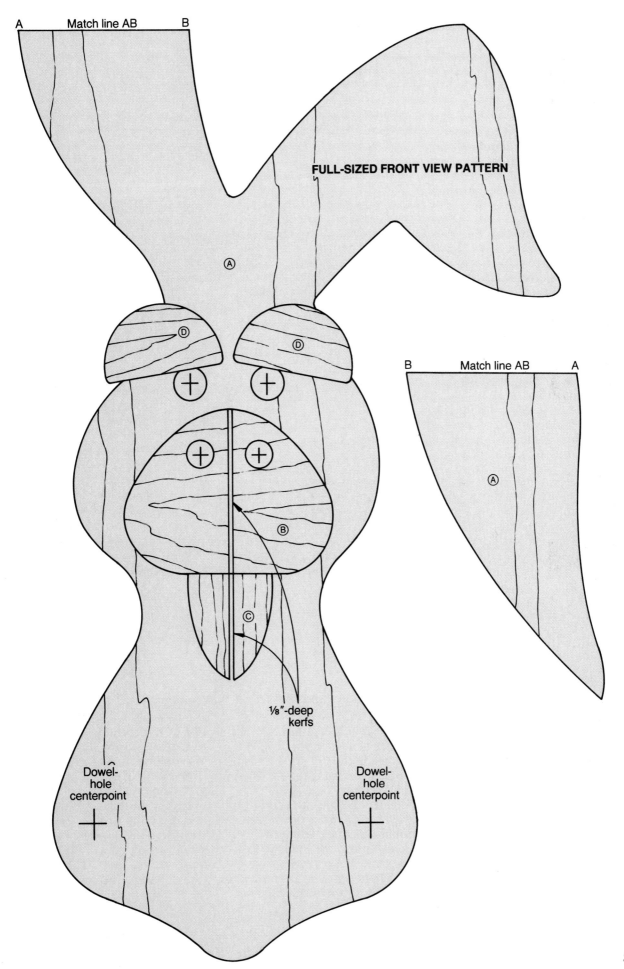

A Match line AB B

FULL-SIZED FRONT VIEW PATTERN

Ⓐ

Ⓓ   Ⓓ

B Match line AB A

Ⓐ

Ⓑ

⅛"-deep
kerfs

Ⓒ

Dowel-
hole
centerpoint

Dowel-
hole
centerpoint

OAK QUILT RACK

Share the beauty of treasured handiwork or a hand-me-down heirloom on this distinctive quilt rack. Practical and attractive, it fits nicely into most home decors.

Form the end sections

1. To form the arches (A), cut two pieces of 1⁵⁄₁₆" oak—often called 6/4 (six-quarter) stock—9×14½". (We edge-joined narrower stock to make the 9" width.)

2. Using double-faced tape, stick the two arch blanks together face-to-face. Run the bottom edge of the arches over a jointer until the two are flush.

3. Draw a 1" grid measuring 9×14" on a piece of paper. Lay out the shape of the arch on the grid, using the Arch Grid, page 92, as a guide. To do this, mark the points where the arch outline crosses each grid line. Then draw a line to connect the points.

Mark the centerpoints for the 1" dowels (E) onto the grid. Apply spray adhesive to the back of the grid, and stick it to the arches. Position the grid so the bottom edge aligns with the bottom edge of the arch blanks.

4. With a scratch awl, indent the wood at each dowel centerpoint on the face of the pattern. You'll use these points to locate and drill the 1" dowel holes later.

5. Cut the arches to shape (cut the top scrap in one piece and save it for use in clamping the end sections together later). With the arches taped together, sand all contoured edges flush with a drum sander. Remove the paper pattern and separate the pieces.

6. Cut four pieces of 1⁵⁄₁₆" oak to 2×19" for the uprights (B). Now, using the full-sized Ends of Upright Drawing, page 92, lay out the ¼" radii and dowel-hole reference lines on each end of the uprights. Cut and drum-sand the uprights to shape. Using the dimensions on the Exploded View Drawing, *opposite,* mark the dowel-hole centerpoints for each ¾" dowel on the inside face of two of the uprights. Keep these two marked uprights together to assemble in the first end section later on.

7. Using the same techniques described in steps 2 through 5, and using the Grid for Half of Base Drawing, page 92, as a guide, lay out, cut, and drum-sand the two bases (C) to shape.

1" holes 9/16" deep

3/8" dowel 2" long

9½"

¾" hole 9/16" deep,
centered from side to side

2"

3/8" dowel 2" long

3/16" shank hole

1½"

21"

1" dowel 28" long

3/8" round-over
on both sides

3/8" hole
1 1/16" deep

3/8" round-over

¾" dowel 28" long

¼" ogee
on both sides

1/8" pilot hole

3/8" hole
1 1/16" deep

3/8" hole
½" deep

10 × 2¼" F.H.

3/8" round-over
No round-over

3/8" plug ½" long

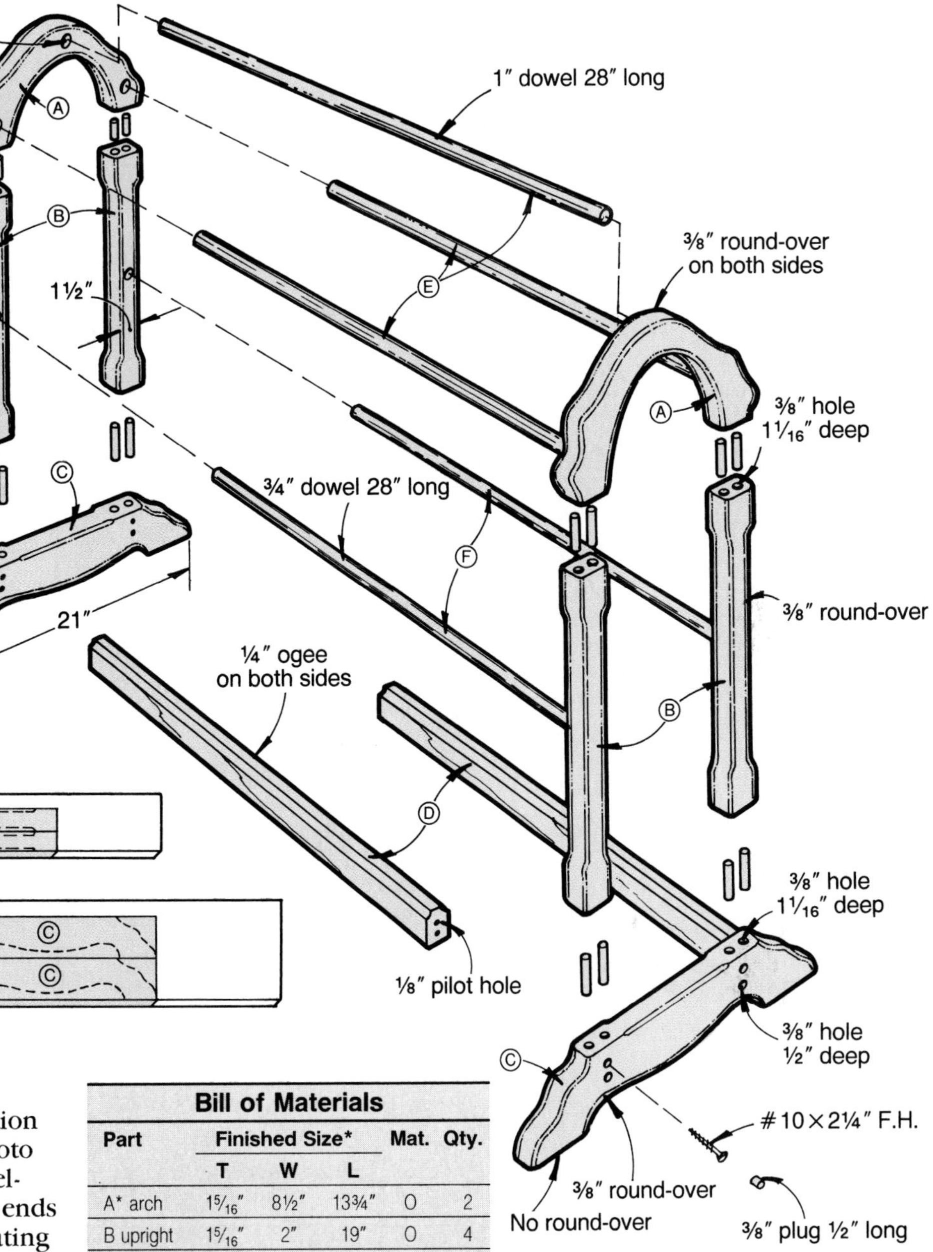

Cutting Diagram

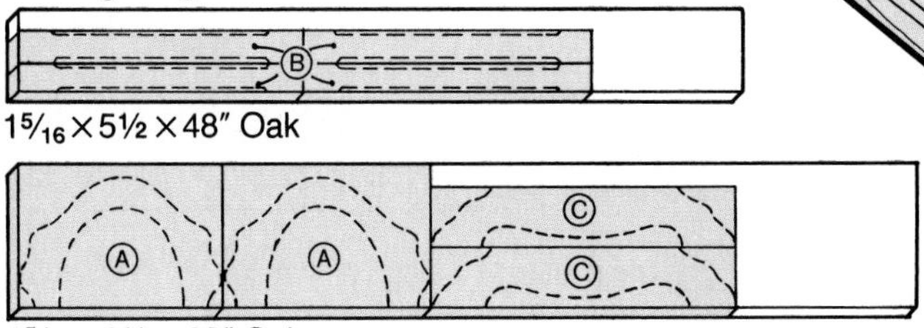

15/16 × 5½ × 48" Oak

15/16 × 9¼ × 60" Oak

Assemble the end sections

1. Dry-clamp each end section together. As shown in the photo on page 93, transfer the dowel-hole reference lines from the ends of each upright onto their mating arch and base pieces. (We used the scrap cutout from the top of each arch and the bottom of each base as straightedges to clamp against.) Labeling the mating pieces at each joint helps speed up assembling each end section later. *continued*

Bill of Materials				
Part	Finished Size*		Mat.	Qty.
	T	W	L		
A* arch	15/16"	8½"	13¾"	O	2
B upright	15/16"	2"	19"	O	4
C* base	15/16"	4"	21"	O	2
D cross member	15/16"	2"	27"	O	2
E upper dowel	1" diam.		28"	OD	3
F lower dowel	¾" diam.		28"	OD	2

*Parts marked with an * are cut larger initially, then trimmed to finished size. Please read the instructions before cutting.

Material Key: O—oak, OD—oak dowel.
Supplies: double-faced tape, paper for grid patterns, spray adhesive, 8—# 10 × 2¼" flathead wood screws, 1" brads, 16—3/8 × 2" dowel pins, stain, finish.

OAK QUILT RACK
continued

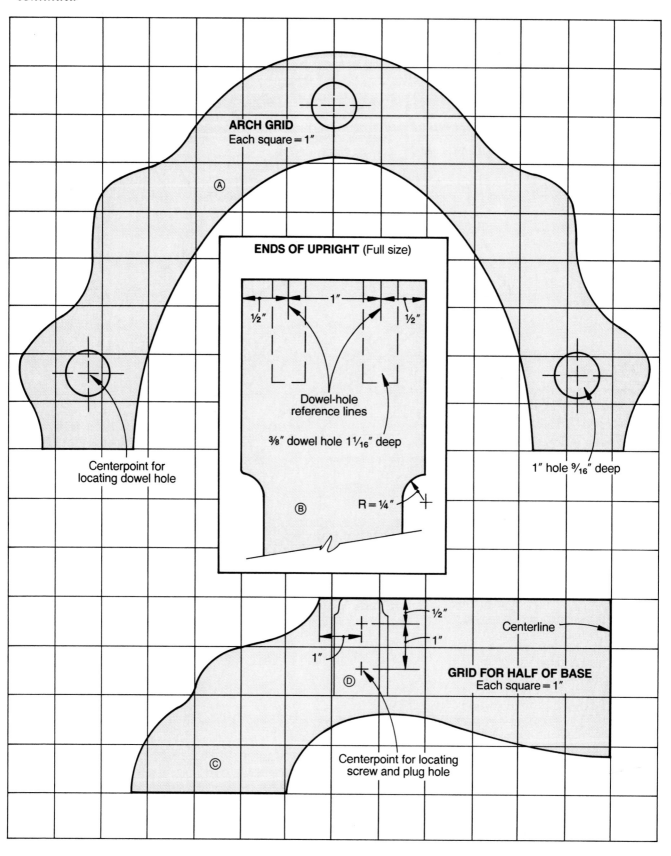

ARCH GRID
Each square = 1″

Ⓐ

ENDS OF UPRIGHT (Full size)

1″

½″   ½″

Dowel-hole
reference lines

⅜″ dowel hole 1¹⁄₁₆″ deep

Ⓑ   R = ¼″

Centerpoint for
locating dowel hole

1″ hole ⁹⁄₁₆″ deep

½″

1″

Centerline

GRID FOR HALF OF BASE
Each square = 1″

1″

Ⓓ

Ⓒ

Centerpoint for locating
screw and plug hole

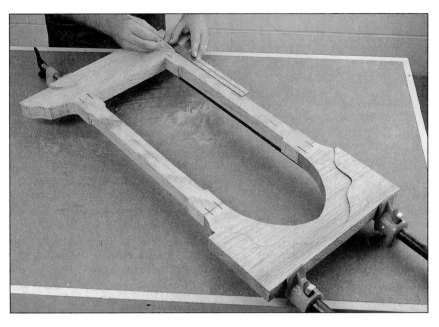

2. Unclamp the end sections. Then, using a doweling jig, drill a pair of ⅜" holes 1¹⁄₁₆" deep where marked at each joint.

3. Cut sixteen ⅜" dowels 2" long. Now glue, dowel, and clamp each end section together.

4. Sand each end section. Rout a ⅜" round-over along all edges, *except* the feet of the bases, where shown on the Exploded View Drawing, page 91.

Assemble the quilt rack

1. Cut the two cross members (D) to size. Next, cut three 1" dowels (E) and two ¾" dowels (F) to finished length (28"). If you have trouble finding oak dowels in your area, see the Buying Guide for a mail-order source.

2. Rout a ¼" ogee along the top edges of both cross members.

3. Snip the head end off a 1" brad, and chuck the brad into your drill. Using the brad as a bit, drill ½"-deep holes (one in each of the two uprights and three in one of the arches) on the centerpoints marked earlier.

Snip the ends off five similar-sized brads so the brads are ⅝" long. Insert a brad in each hole

you just drilled. Place the inside of the second end section facedown on top of the other end section. Align the bottom and side edges. Press the two end sections together to transfer the dowel-hole centerpoints as shown in the drawing at *lower left*.

4. Separate the end sections and remove the brads. Finally, drill a 1" hole ⁹⁄₁₆" deep for each 1" dowel (E) and ¾" holes ⁹⁄₁₆" deep for each ¾" dowel (F), using the brad holes and indentations in each end section as guides.

5. Dry-clamp the quilt rack together with the dowels and cross members in position (note on the grid drawing that the top edge of the cross members aligns flush with the top edge of each base). Now, using the hole sizes shown on the Exploded View Drawing, drill plug, shank, and pilot holes through each base (C) and into the ends of each of the cross members.

6. Glue and clamp the rack with all cross members and dowels in place between the end sections. Remove any excess glue after a tough skin forms. Fasten the cross members to the bases with #10 × 2¼" flathead wood screws.

7. Plane a thicker piece of oak to ⁹⁄₁₆" thick. Cut ⅜" plugs ⁹⁄₁₆" long from the oak. Plug the screw holes and sand the plugs flush.

Finish the rack

1. Finish-sand and apply the stain and finish. (We applied a walnut stain and polyurethane.)

Buying Guide

● **Oak dowels.** 1"-diameter dowel 36" long (3 needed), catalog no. 20974. ¾"-diameter dowel 36" long (2 needed), catalog no. 20966. To find out the current prices, write The Woodworkers' Store, 21801 Industrial Blvd., Rogers, MN 55374-9514. Or call 612/428-2199.

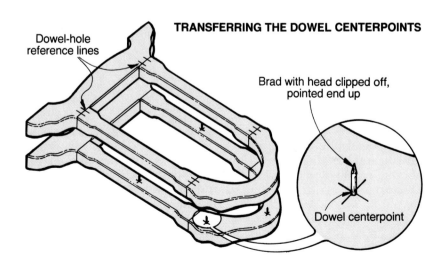

TRANSFERRING THE DOWEL CENTERPOINTS

Dowel-hole reference lines

Brad with head clipped off, pointed end up

Dowel centerpoint

BENTWOOD COAT TREE

To test your bentwood lamination skills, you won't find a better project than this sturdy coat tree, with its curved uprights of resawed oak strips. Be sure to save the bending form when you're finished—you can bet that friends will ask you to make duplicate coat trees for *their* houses.

Build the form

1. Cut the pieces for the form to size and shape as dimensioned on the Bending Form Drawing, *opposite, top.* Glue and stack the particleboard strips to form the sections used to shape the upright (A, B, C, D). Sand smooth the surface of the particleboard that will come in contact with the oak strips, and screw the sections to the particleboard base.

2. Using a fine-toothed handsaw, cut through the particleboard strips to form the cutoff guides shown in the drawing. (The guides will be used later for trimming the ends of the laminations.) Chamfer both ends of the base so they run parallel to the strips.

Laminate the uprights

1. Rip ten 2⅛"-wide strips from ¾"-thick oak stock that's at least 7' long. Crosscut each of the 2⅛" strips to 78".

2. Resaw the strips (the stock will be on edge) to ⅛" thick. (You'll end up with more than the required 24 thin strips—six for each upright—but you'll probably break a few when resawing and bending.) Then mark the lengthwise center of each strip.

EXPLODED VIEW

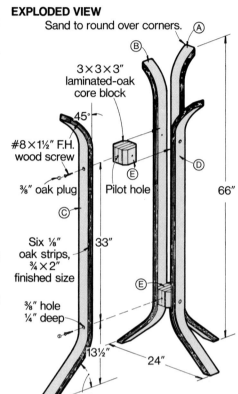

Sand to round over corners. Ⓐ

Ⓑ

3×3×3" laminated-oak core block

45°

#8×1½" F.H. wood screw

⅜" oak plug

Ⓒ

Six ⅛" oak strips, ¾×2" finished size

⅜" hole ¼" deep

Ⓓ

Ⓔ Pilot hole

Ⓔ

66"

33"

13½"

45°

24"

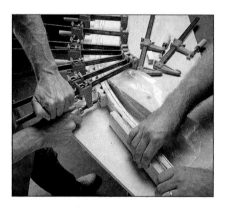

3. Lay waxed paper on the form, then glue and clamp six thin strips to the form to laminate the longest upright (A) as shown in the photo, *above.* Make sure the center marks on the form and the strips line up. (We poured woodworker's glue [yellow glue]

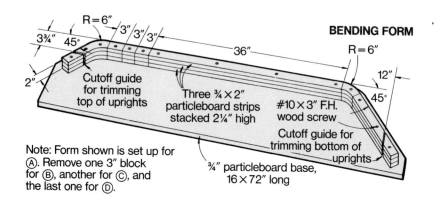

BENDING FORM

R=6"
3¾" 45°
R=6"
3"/3"/3"
36"
12"
45°
2"

Cutoff guide for trimming top of uprights

Three ¾ × 2" particleboard strips stacked 2¼" high

#10 × 3" F.H. wood screw

Cutoff guide for trimming bottom of uprights

Note: Form shown is set up for Ⓐ. Remove one 3" block for Ⓑ, another for Ⓒ, and the last one for Ⓓ.

¾" particleboard base, 16 × 72" long

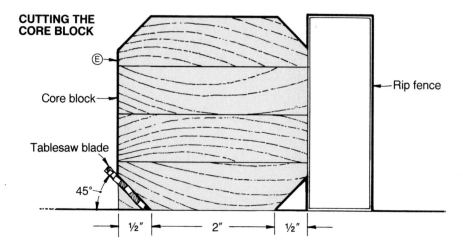

CUTTING THE CORE BLOCK

Ⓔ

Core block

Tablesaw blade

Rip fence

45°

½" — 2" — ½"

into a paint tray and applied it to the strips with a narrow paint roller. We also found it handy to have a helper when bending the wood around the curves.)

4. After the glue dries, remove the laminated upright from the form, and get rid of the waxed paper clinging to the upright. Reclamp the upright to the form, making sure that the top edge of the upright is slightly above the top edge of the form. Use only enough clamps to hold the lamination in place. Scrape the excess glue from the top edge of the lamination, and use a hand plane or a belt sander to smooth the edge. Check the edge

periodically with a small combination square to ensure squareness; sand the edge smooth. Flip the lamination over and repeat this process with the other edge, planing the upright down to a 2" finished width.

5. Using a fine-toothed handsaw, trim both ends of the upright using the cutoff guides shown on the Bending Form Drawing, *top*.

6. Remove one of the 3" sections from the form. Then reposition the curved portion of the form so that it fits snugly against the center section, and

rescrew it to the base. (Save the 3" piece if you plan to reuse the form later.) Now repeat the procedure to make the second-longest upright (B).

7. Laminate the remaining two uprights (C, D), following the same procedure. Don't forget to remove another 3" section from the form each time.

8. Sand the ends of each upright to round over the sharp edges as shown on the Exploded View Drawing, *opposite*. Then, using sandpaper, break the edges and finish-sand all four uprights.

Form the core blocks

1. Cut four pieces of ¾" oak 3¼ × 10". Glue and clamp the pieces together. After the glue dries, scrape off the excess and plane, joint, or rip the lamination to 3 × 3 × 10".

2. Using the Cutting the Core Block Drawing, *left*, as a guide, cut the chamfers at each corner of the lamination with a tablesaw. Crosscut the lamination into two 3"-long blocks (E). Sand both blocks.

Assemble the coat tree

1. Glue and clamp two opposing uprights (A, C) to the core blocks, keeping the bottom of the uprights level. Drill ⅜" holes ¼" deep into the uprights where shown on the Exploded View Drawing. Then drill a pilot hole through the center of each hole into the core block for the #8 × 1½" wood screws. Fasten all four uprights to the core blocks in this manner.

2. Cut ⅜" oak plugs, glue them into the holes over the screws, and sand the plugs flush. Apply the finish. (We used a small foam brush to apply polyurethane. It came in handy when coating the inside of the uprights.)

ACKNOWLEDGMENTS

Project Designers

Dave Ashe—Burl-Topped Hallway Shelf, pages 5–7; Traditional-Style Hall Table, pages 34–37

Janet Betts—Rabbit Clothes Rack, pages 88–89

Jim Boelling—Filigree Plant Stand, pages 8–11; Pedestal Display Stand, pages 16–18; Pint-Size Picture Frame, pages 19–21; Tabletop Easel, pages 26–29

Arnold Davison—Collector's Showcase, pages 12–15

James R. Downing—Stacked-Molding Picture Frame, pages 22–25; Waterfall End Table, pages 38–40; Burl-Topped Coffee Table, pages 41–45; Plastic-Laminate Parsons Table, pages 46–49; Angelfish Wall Clock, pages 59–60; Turned Teak Timepiece, pages 62–63; Torchère Floor Lamp, pages 66–71; Chippendale Wall Mirror, pages 72–75; Fishing Rod Rack, pages 84–87; Bentwood Coat Tree, pages 94–95

Paul Foster—Contemporary Coffee Table, pages 31–33

Wes Gard—Oak Quilt Rack, pages 90–93

Gary Hood—Contemporary Coffee Table, pages 31–33

Marlen Kemmet—Freestanding Wine Rack, pages 81–83

Jim Payne—Wenge Wall Clock, pages 64–65

Ralph Peterman—Art Deco Mantel Clock, page 61

Bob Sellers—Kid-Size Picnic Table, pages 50–51

Jay Taylor—Oak Magazine Rack, pages 77–80

Inga Vesterby—Walnut Jewelry Case, pages 53–58

Photographers

Bob Calmer
Al Elder
Hopkins Associates
Jim Kascoutas

Illustrators

Kim Downing
Randall Foshee
Mike Henry
Bill Zaun

If you would like to order any additional copies of our books, call 1-800-678-2803 or check with your local bookstore.
